Surviving Stalking

Surviving Stalking is a practical and comprehensive survival manual for victims of stalking and related crimes. It offers sound, realistic, practical advice to victims and also gives guidance through each of the criminal justice processes in America, Britain and Australia. Using case descriptions, Michele Pathé describes the traumatic effects of stalking, the course of these symptoms and how best to obtain psychological care and support. It is the first comprehensive book for a general readership providing a contemporary account of types of victim, types of stalker, stalkers' motives, strategies to prevent and overcome stalking and a list of the resources available to victims of stalking.

Surviving Stalking will be of great interest not only to those who have been or are being stalked but also to health, law enforcement and legal professionals who work with stalkers and their victims.

Michele Pathé is Consultant Forensic Psychiatrist at the Victorian Institute of Forensic Mental Health, Melbourne, where she has been treating stalkers in the world's first clinical outpatient programme since the early 1990s. She is co-director of the Stalking and Threat Management Centre in Melbourne. She is co-author of the best selling *Stalkers and their Victims*, winner of the American Psychiatric Association's Guttmacher award for an outstanding contribution to the literature on forensic psychiatry.

Surviving Stalking

Michele Pathé

CAMBRIDGE
UNIVERSITY PRESS

PUBLISHED BY THE PRESS SYNDICATE OF THE UNIVERSITY OF CAMBRIDGE
The Pitt Building, Trumpington Street, Cambridge, United Kingdom

CAMBRIDGE UNIVERSITY PRESS
The Edinburgh Building, Cambridge CB2 2RU, UK
40 West 20th Street, New York, NY 10011–4211, USA
477 Williamstown Road, Port Melbourne, VIC 3207, Australia
Ruiz de Alarcón 13, 28014 Madrid, Spain
Dock House, The Waterfront, Cape Town 8001, South Africa

http://www.cambridge.org

© Cambridge University Press 2002

First published 2002

Printed in the United Kingdom at the University Press, Cambridge

Typeface Minion 11/14.5 pt   *System* QuarkXPress™   [S E]

A catalogue record for this book is available from the British Library

Library of Congress Cataloguing in Publication data

Pathé, Michele, 1959–
  Surviving stalking / Michele Pathé.
    p.   cm.
  Includes bibliographical references and index.
  ISBN 0 521 00964 2 (pb.)
  1. Stalking.   2. Stalking victims.   3. Stalkers.   I. Title.

  HV6594.P37   2002
  362.88–dc21   2001052720

ISBN 0 521 00964 2 paperback

Every effort has been made in preparing this book to provide accurate and up-to-date information which is in accord with accepted standards and practice at the time of publication. Nevertheless, the authors, editors and publisher can make no warranties that the information contained herein is totally free from error, not least because clinical standards are constantly changing through research and regulation. The authors, editors and publisher therefore disclaim all liability for direct or consequential damages resulting from the use of material contained in this book. Readers are strongly advised to pay careful attention to information provided by the manufacturer of any drugs or equipment that they plan to use.

Although case histories are drawn from actual cases, every effort has been made to disguise the identities of the individuals involved.

Contents

Acknowledgments

Many thanks to my colleagues and co-researchers Professor Paul Mullen and Dr Rosie Purcell for their substantial contribution and support. Thank you to the friends and colleagues who provided helpful feedback and advice, in particular Dr Edward Petch and Dr Doreen Orion. I am also grateful to Detective Inspectors Ian Smith and Linda Dawson of the Hampshire Constabulary, Tracey Morgan and Mohini Sethi for their assistance with the preparation of the UK chapter and appendices, and to Rebecca Metcalfe, Victim Witness Unit, and prosecutor Kathy Delgado at the Boulder County District Attorney's Office. Finally, I am indebted to the many stalking victims and their families whose stories inspired this book. May we all learn from the injuries and injustices they have suffered.

Introduction

In the space of a decade, the word 'stalking' has acquired a new meaning and significance in our vocabulary. Most people are acquainted with its contemporary use, either through various depictions in the media or through personal knowledge of someone exposed to the unwanted attentions of a stalker. The term 'stalking' has been used since ancient times to refer both to the act of following one's prey and to walk stealthily, but it was only in the late 1980s that the media coined the word to describe the persistent pestering and harassment of celebrities by fans. Use of the term has been progressively expanded to encompass the behaviours of those who harass previous partners, fellow workers, acquaintances and a range of other ordinary people. The behaviour itself is not new, but *labelling* it and acknowledging it as an important social problem has enabled us to recognize and act upon it.

Our understanding of stalking is still evolving. There is not much published work on the subject, and much of it offers little in the way of practical solutions to the problem. Research is gathering momentum, however, generating some insights into the nature of stalking, its frequency, and the characteristics and motives of those who stalk and the people they target. These studies lend support to burgeoning clinical impressions that stalking can have serious ramifications for the victim and those who are less directly involved, as well as for stalkers themselves and society as a whole.

In the popular press there has been a tendency to sensationalize cases of stalking, especially when they involve public figures such as film stars and politicians. We are regularly bombarded with the most severe and bizarre images from the range of stalking experiences. There is no denying such cases exist, nor their importance in highlighting to the rest of society and the criminal justice system the potential dangers of stalking and the plight of stalking victims. However, this book has a practical focus, providing victims of stalking and affected third parties with essential information and advice that will enable them to withstand and ultimately end their stalker's intrusions. It endeavours to present a more balanced and representative portrayal of the crime of stalking without the usual potpourri of disturbing worst case scenarios. For the interested reader there is an abundance of case material to be found among the references listed in the reading guide.

Stalking victims, their families and the wider community often ask why a person stalks. It is a popular misconception that there is a universal stalker profile with a single motive. This book describes five broad categories of stalker based on the stalker's probable motivation and the context in which the stalking arises. Most stalking victims will recognize the category to which their stalker belongs, although the groups are not mutually exclusive and it is possible for stalkers to share features of more than one category. The utility of a classification system is that it enables us to make certain predictions, such as the likely duration of the stalking, the likelihood of violence and approaches to management.

People who are directly or indirectly targeted by a stalker are naturally concerned about the stalker's propensity for violence, whether aimed at the victim or their loved ones, pets or property. Although the risk of violence is fortunately small, certain factors that may enhance this risk have been identified. Chapter 4 outlines the characteristics of stalkers that have been associated with a greater likelihood of aggression.

Victims often question whether they could have 'seen it coming' or whether the harassment could have been avoided had they recognized the warning signs at an earlier stage and responded in a different manner. Their self recriminations may be fuelled by criticism from a number of quarters for appearing to *encourage* the stalker's attentions or for what others perceive as a failure to take more assertive action. Ultimately, many victims feel blamed and ashamed. This book identifies features that can alert individuals to potential stalkers and strategies for responding to them. There will, unfortunately, be many instances in which it is not possible to prevent victimization, although there are always steps that can be taken to discourage stalkers early in the course of their pursuit. It is important to recognize that victims of stalking are no more to blame for their predicament than victims of most other crimes, regardless of the nature of their relationships to the stalkers. I hope that this book will enlighten those who sit in judgement on stalking victims and encourage them to become constructive participants in the victims' defence plans.

Victims and their loved ones are anxious to know if their reaction to their ordeal is 'normal' or whether they are 'going insane'. Most of us who view the impact of stalking second hand have little difficulty appreciating the basis for the traumatic stress symptoms that stalking victims commonly manifest. However, the victims themselves – after what may be protracted periods of harassment, attitudes of disbelief and trivialization that they encounter and the impotence of the 'system' to intervene – begin to question whether it is actually they who have got it wrong. Have they over-reacted, are they dreaming or have they lost their grip on reality? Are they so unworthy that their anguish should be regarded with such indifference? Many who succumb to stalking have no previous experience of significant emotional upheaval or psychiatric symptoms of a severity that necessitated medical attention. They have typically been socially active, well adjusted individuals. As a direct consequence of being stalked they become anxious, moody and withdrawn. Their functioning at work and in close personal relationships may deteriorate. Not uncommonly, victims admit to thoughts of harming their stalkers or even themselves, because they come to view these desperate measures as the only means of escaping their ordeals. This book examines the impact of stalking on the lives of victims. The information is also a useful guide for the friends and families of stalking victims, many of whom feel alarmed and perplexed by the change in their loved ones. Through an improved understanding of stalking and its effects, families can advance from a position of angry ineffectuality to providers of constructive support and co-strategists in the primary victim's fight against the stalker.

Despite advances in our understanding of this menace to society, much has yet to be learned about stalking. Considerably more must be done to optimize support for victims. This will also assist in the identification of stalkers and the control of their criminal activities through the appropriate mix of treatment and legal sanctions. Unfortunately, since there is no training that can prepare the average person for a stalker's invasion, few victims have a response plan or even a list of services that can be relied on to intervene effectively. Unlike the process in place for victims of, for example, workplace injuries, crime victims in general are either unaware of the services available to meet their needs, or they approach a bewildering range of agencies in a largely ad hoc fashion. Too many stalking victims who, quite reasonably, appeal to 'helping' services such as the police, the legal system or the medical profession encounter attitudes of indifference, disbelief and conflicting, if not counterproductive, advice. Effective management of stalking requires the education, co-operation and co-ordination of law makers, law enforcers, the judiciary, treatment services and, importantly, stalking victims. This book is intended to help victims and those whose lives are indirectly affected by stalking, to negotiate the maze of services and strategies that confront them in their quest for a successful resolution.

Knowledge is an essential tool in the stalking victim's armament. In addition to the information summarized in this survival manual, the material cited in the reading guide provides more in depth accounts of various aspects of stalking. These publications have been recommended by stalking victims and those whose work brings them into contact with stalkers and stalking victims. The authors cited throughout this book are indexed in the reference list that precedes the reading guide.

The information in these pages is necessarily prosaic and concise. The pervasive stress of being stalked can have a profound effect on a victim's capacity for concentration and sustained attention. This impedes his or her ability to assimilate the contents of more detailed publications. Accordingly, the important points in Chapters 1 to 7 are summarized at the end of each chapter. Chapters 8 to 13 provide important practical information which is best read in its entirety. Again, the reading guide provides more detailed information for the interested reader.

For simplicity, this book refers to the targets of stalkers as 'victims'. Although some may be offended by this term because it implies a degree of helplessness and powerlessness on the victim's part, this is precisely what the object of a stalker's pursuit experiences. The purpose of this book is to help victims become survivors, but while they are being stalked they are indisputably victims. Although people who are stalked can *become* survivors, they do not start out that way. Also, we now know that most stalkers are male and most stalking victims are female. For convenience, this book uses the male pronoun for stalkers and the female pronoun for stalking victims, but it is not my intention to deny the existence of female stalkers or the distress and disruption that stalking creates in the lives of male victims.

My colleagues and I at the Victorian Institute of Forensic Mental Health in Melbourne, Australia, have been assessing and treating stalkers and victims of stalking since the early 1990s. The case examples in this book are based on our combined clinical experience, but identifying information has been altered to protect the identities of those involved. The advice to victims contained in these pages is derived from our clinical understanding of stalking behaviour, major research findings and our discussions with experts in the areas of criminal justice and personal protection. It is also drawn from the collective wisdom of other clinicians and academics in the field, whose publications appear in the reading guide. Most importantly, this book has emerged in response to the comments and expressed needs of the hundreds of stalking victims who have consulted us over the years. For many of these the path to freedom and the reclamation of their lives was strewn with obstacles, ignorance and much unnecessary pain. All share the hope that others might learn from their ordeal, so that the suffering of future stalking victims may be alleviated or prevented altogether.

1

What is stalking?

Legal definition

'Stalking' may be a new word in its current context, but the behaviour itself has long been recognized in criminal justice circles. Indeed, it has been dealt with in various ways since at least the eighteenth century. Existing laws relied, however, on prosecuting stalking *related* crimes such as trespass, breaking and entering, criminal damage and threats to kill. By the end of the 1980s it was becoming increasingly clear that these laws were inadequate in deterring stalkers and protecting their victims.

Rather than modify existing laws to deal with this complex crime, legislators throughout many Western nations moved to specifically criminalize stalking. The impetus for developing the first stalking laws was the tragic murder in 1989 of American sitcom actress Rebecca Schaeffer (*My Sister Sam*) by the disordered fan and stalker Robert Bardo. A flood of stalking legislation has emerged over the past decade, beginning in California in 1991 and extending to the rest of the United States of America, Canada, Australia, the United Kingdom and New Zealand. Similar laws are now being considered or enacted in continental Europe and parts of Asia.

The framing of legislation has been confounded by the problem of defining a criminal activity that comprises a series of actions each of which, when taken individually, may constitute legitimate behaviour (e.g. sending flowers or waiting outside a person's workplace). In creating a legal definition of stalking, legislators have broadly prohibited contacts and communications that occur on *two or more occasions* and which evoke fear in the target.

The legal definition of stalking or criminal harassment varies according to jurisdiction. Although there is no consensus, the behaviours covered by the legislation are broadly similar from one jurisdiction to the next. It is wise to familiarize yourself with the stalking laws in your particular jurisdiction. In the US and Australia they can be obtained by contacting your state attorney general's office or, in the UK, the Lord Chancellor's office or website. The legislation is also available for perusal at university law libraries. The acts are mostly short 'plain English' documents unencumbered by the complexity and longwindedness that characterize older pieces of legislation. Whether these laws prove adequate in effectively preventing and punishing stalking remains to be seen, and much will depend on the willingness of the criminal justice system to view the offence seriously.

Critical elements of successful stalking laws include their capacity to provide immediate and effective protection for the victim and the appropriate combination of legal sanctions and treatment for the stalker, aimed at preventing a recurrence of the behaviour. Existing stalking laws, though not without their critics, have already proved a significant advance. Used properly, the legislation has spared victims from having to wait until the stalker actually attacks and injures them or damages their property before the police can intervene. Unfortunately some police officers remain ignorant of this important reform. *It is vital that victims know the stalking provisions in their jurisdiction and ensure that the police are also familiar with these provisions.*

Clinical definition

Unlike legal definitions of stalking, which are designed to prosecute criminal behaviour, other definitions have emerged which are aimed at developing our understanding of this phenomenon and its clinical management. Clinicians and researchers have defined stalking as:

A constellation of behaviours involving repeated and persistent attempts to impose on another person unwanted communication and/or contact.   (Mullen et al., 1999)

These behaviours are typically experienced as intrusive and cause the victim concern or fear. Indeed, it is not the intentions of the *stalker* that defines a stalking incident but the reactions of the individual or individuals who are targeted. Stalkers can communicate with their victim in a number of ways:

Phone calls

This is one of the commonest forms of harassment, the phone being an easy and accessible tool for intruding on others. Calls are typically received at the victim's home or workplace, or both. The caller may remain silent, hang up when the victim answers, plead for a relationship or reconciliation, threaten, cajole or utter obscenities. Calls may be incessant, stalkers often choosing inconvenient times such as late at night. Some stalkers call to describe what the victims are wearing, or they may phone the victims at other venues, such as restaurants or conferences, or even at the victims' holiday destination, deliberately conveying to the victims that they are under surveillance.

Case example

Jeanette, a legal secretary, was repeatedly approached by a male patron at her local gym. She tried to escape the man's unwanted attentions by forfeiting her gym membership, but he then repeatedly phoned her at her home and workplace. He insisted they go on a date, but she firmly and consistently declined. The phone calls escalated, such that her employers complained that her 'boyfriend' was obstructing legitimate calls. Jeanette was subjected to the man's tearful pleading at all hours, starting the moment she entered her apartment at the end of the day. She obtained an unlisted phone number, but within a week this had been unwittingly divulged to the stalker by a work colleague. Alarmed, sleep deprived and on the verge of losing her job, Jeanette contacted the police. They warned the man that his behaviour constituted stalking and that any future intrusions would be prosecuted. Jeanette received no further communications from her would-be suitor.

Letters and cards

These are usually posted or hand delivered to the victim's home or workplace. Occasionally, notes are attached to the victim's property such as the car. The author may conceal his identity. The content of letters, like phone calls, can be romantic or threatening or a mixture of the two. These communications may also be sent to third parties, either because they are perceived as hindering access to the victim or as a means of spreading malicious gossip about the victim.

Facsimiles

These are most often sent to the victim's workplace. The stalker may attempt to embarrass the victim by faxing scandalous messages that can be read by co-workers.

The Internet

Repeated threats or harassing behaviour over the Internet, email, chat rooms, newsgroups or other electronic communications are now commonly referred to as 'cyberstalking'. Victims may be flooded with messages ('mail bombing'), obstructing legitimate communications. As access to email increases, particularly in work settings, so too do the opportunities for stalkers to abuse it. Electronic communications offer them anonymity, through the use of anonymous remailers (an online service that masks the sender's identity), and opportunities to access computers in public domains (e.g. Internet cafés or public libraries).

Some individuals unwittingly encourage the attentions of a cyberstalker by posting home pages loaded with personal information. Online stalking can become particularly problematic (and potentially physically dangerous) when the perpetrator, armed with his victim's naively imparted personal details, continues his pursuit offline.

Graffiti

Stalkers may adorn the victims' homes or cars with messages, usually declarations of love or hostility or malicious allegations.

Unwanted gifts or other materials

There seems no end to the creativity of some stalkers in their choice of gifts. They vary from the predictable (chocolates, soft toys, flowers, books and jewellery) to the bizarre (jars of urine and frozen chickens) and the macabre (dead pets and funeral notices). Some stalkers send only one or two such gifts whereas others send gifts, typically flowers, by the truckload.

Case example

Carol, a high school teacher, was pursued anonymously over a six week period. She received 'gifts' through the internal mail at work, the first a parcel containing flower seedlings and a can of tomato soup. Some weeks later she received a homemade chocolate cake and an assortment of women's magazines. Two months later, following a series of 'hang-up' calls, a packet of tampons was deposited in her letter box at home. Carol found the bizarre and inexplicable nature of this material and the anonymity of its sender extremely disturbing. She could not continue teaching because 'every student in the class was potentially my stalker'.

Stalkers make contact with their victims by means of one or more of the following methods:

Following

Stalkers commonly follow their victims, and to a lesser extent other parties, on foot, bicycle or by motor vehicle, enabling them to materialize at various venues attended by the victims.

Approaching

Some victims note the ubiquitous appearance of the stalkers, encountering them at shopping centres, while on outings with friends and even at family funerals or their children's school functions. While some stalkers merely observe from a distance, others will approach their victims and try to engage them in conversation.

Maintaining surveillance

Some stalkers wait and watch at locations frequented by the victims, occasionally enlisting the help of others to share shifts. Surveillance may occur from any number of vantage points, usually from the stalker's car or outside the victim's home.

The stalker may engage in associated behaviours, including the following:

Ordering goods or services on the victim's behalf

The commonest example is the late night pizza delivery. Taxis, fire trucks and ambulances have all been called to the homes of stalking victims. Stalkers have also *cancelled* services on the victims' behalf, including their electricity and gas supplies.

Initiating spurious legal action against the victim

It is not uncommon for stalkers to force their victims to court in order to have contact with them. Legal action may in other cases be motivated predominantly by a desire for revenge.

Case example

Ross, a divorced accountant, was stalked by a young woman with whom he had had a brief affair. Furious at his rejection of her, the woman repeatedly approached him and castigated him in public and at work and made frequent abusive and threatening phone calls. Ross obtained a protective injunction that prohibited her from making any further contact. The woman promptly appealed against the injunction, forcing Ross to return to court to face his former lover. She represented herself in the hearing, clearly revelling in the opportunity to cross examine her hapless victim. Ross ultimately retained the injunction, but he regarded the hearing as a terrible violation and blatant manipulation of the criminal justice system.

Spreading false rumours to discredit the victim

The stalker may attempt to tarnish the victim's reputation by spreading malicious rumours among the victim's friends, relatives, work colleagues and neighbours. Some victims have been reported to government agencies for alleged social security fraud or child abuse, causing the victim great distress despite the ultimate dismissal of the claims.

Threats

These may be explicit or implied and often involve threats of physical violence or promises to discredit or publicly humiliate the victim. Threats may also be directed at other parties such as the victim's family, friends, co-workers or pets.

Damage to property and pets

Property usually targeted includes the victim's car, with tyres being slashed or deflated, paintwork scratched and fuel lines severed. Stalkers may also damage gardens, tamper with letter boxes or emblazon fences with graffiti. Some break into their victims' homes to leave notes or to steal personal items such as address books or photographs. A few stalkers injure or kill family pets.

Assault

A minority of stalkers do proceed to assault their victim or third parties. In most cases the attack is preceded by threats. Assaults may be physical or, much less commonly, sexual in nature. Occasionally, the victim's partner, family or friends are targeted, particularly when they are perceived as obstructing the stalker's pursuit. Chapter 4 discusses factors associated with stalker violence.

Stalking by proxy

Most stalkers act alone. Sometimes, however, others may be persuaded to perpetuate the harassment. This is generally achieved by deceit. For example, the stalker may recruit a friend to spy on the victim because, he alleges, the victim is 'cheating' on him. It is rare for stalkers to pay the substantial fees required by private detectives in order to track down their victims or to bribe others to assist in the pursuit of the victims. It is particularly rare for stalkers to co-opt large networks of people to harass the objects of their attention, although victims who are experiencing considerable stress may come to fear this is the case. If you are concerned about stalking on this distressing scale you are strongly urged to seek medical help.

Summary

- Stalking is a new label for behaviour that has almost certainly existed for centuries.
- Stalking legislation originated in the USA in 1991 and many Western nations have since followed suit.
- Stalking laws have been an important advance, but they are still underused and inconsistently enforced.
- Be familiar with the stalking laws in your jurisdiction.
- Clinically, stalking refers to a range of behaviours involving repeated and persistent attempts to impose on another person unwanted communication or contact, or both. The behaviours are intrusive and elicit concern or fear in the victim.

2

How common is stalking?

The prevalence of stalking depends on how we define it. For instance, stalking defined as any unwanted contact will be a far more common experience than a definition confining it to specific patterns of repeatedly intrusive behaviours which evoke fear. It is also dependent on the sample in which stalking prevalence is being measured. One might expect rates of stalking to be higher when the group studied is comprised of victims of domestic violence compared with a sample of the community chosen at random.

'Prevalence' refers to the proportion of the population who, at a given time, have the experience in question. To date, studies of the prevalence of stalking have essentially been studies of the prevalence of *victims' reports of being stalked*. Stalkers seldom disclose their behaviours when surveyed, assurances of anonymity notwithstanding. (This is perhaps a reflection of the poor insight of some stalkers into the impact of their activities as much as any deliberate evasion; more on that in Chapter 3).

There are remarkably few published studies that have examined the prevalence and nature of stalking in the community. The first of these was conducted in Australia in 1996 by the Australian Bureau of Statistics (ABS) (Australian Bureau of Statistics, 1996). This was a national survey of women's broader experiences of physical and sexual violence, and it included questions related to stalking and harassment. In a randomly selected community sample of 6300 adult women each was asked in a confidential interview whether they had ever been 'stalked' by a man, the definition of stalking being based on a composite of stalking laws in Australia. The survey found that 15% of women acknowledged being stalked by a man at some time in their lives, which would imply that an estimated one million Australian women have experienced stalking on this scale. A further 2.4% said they had been stalked in the 12 months before the survey, almost a quarter of whom were experiencing ongoing harassment.

The frequency of stalking reported in the ABS survey is likely to be an underestimate given that victimization of *men* and same gender stalking (i.e. women pursued by *women*) were not considered. The study did, however, define stalking rather loosely and the experience of fear was not necessary to qualify as a victim. This may have resulted in the inclusion of isolated, inadvertent behaviours that do not constitute stalking, such as following someone in traffic.

The US National Institute of Justice (Tjaden and Thoennes, 1998) overcame some of the shortcomings of the ABS survey when it commissioned a study specifically to examine the extent of stalking within the wider community. Importantly, the design incorporated male as well as female subjects. It used a representative random sample of 8000 women and 8000 men from across the USA, all of who participated in telephone based interviews. The study revealed that 8% of women and 2% of men had experienced stalking at some time in their lives. When the only requirement to qualify as a stalking victim was that the subject experienced behaviour that caused them to feel a *little* fear, as opposed to being significantly frightened or fearful of bodily harm, the prevalence of victimization increased from 8% to 12% in women, and from 2% to 4% among men.

Initial results from a 1999 random community survey conducted in Melbourne, Australia (Purcell et al., 2002) involving 3700 adults drawn from the electoral roll suggests the prevalence of stalking may be even higher. A third of those sampled had experienced at least two unwanted stalking behaviours. Over 10% reported 10 or more intrusions that were moderately frightening or worse.

The 1998 British Crime Survey (Budd and Mattinson, 2000) involving nearly 10 000 people in England and Wales found that 16% of women and 7% of men had been subject to persistent and unwanted attention at some time in their lives, and almost 3% of the sample reported they were stalked in the preceding 12 months. This equated to 880 000 victims throughout the country.

The findings from these first community surveys confirm a growing impression that, at least in English speaking nations, stalking is not uncommon. Furthermore, there is remarkable consistency in the patterns and methods of pursuit reported by victims in these studies. Most subjects experienced following and surveillance, and telephone and postal harassment were also common. Behaviours such as destruction of property and pets were less common, as were explicit threats to harm the victim or other parties. In most cases the stalking ended after several months.

   Further large scale studies are underway. These seek to gauge more accurately the extent of this crime in our community and ultimately to develop a better understanding of stalkers and their management.

Summary

- The prevalence and nature of stalking in the community have not received extensive study.
- The largest survey to date, conducted by the US National Institute of Justice, found that 8% of women and 2% of men had experienced stalking at some time in their lives.
- These studies indicate that stalking is not uncommon.
- Patterns of harassment reported by victims are quite consistent across studies (following and surveillance being most common, then harassment by telephone and letters).
- The duration of stalking does not persist beyond a few months in most of the cases identified in community surveys.

3

Who stalks?

Stalking is not the exclusive domain of either gender, but in most studies to date around 80% of stalkers have been male. People of any age from teenagers to octogenarians can stalk, but those in their thirties most commonly engage in the behaviour. Many stalkers are unemployed, some as a direct result of their all-consuming pursuit of their victim, but a significant minority are professionally employed or hold other responsible positions. Over half of all stalkers studied have never experienced a long term relationship, and a third are separated or divorced.

Stalking, like any form of complex human behaviour, can be the product of a number of different states of mind. An Australian study of 145 stalkers (Mullen et al., 1999) found that while the majority were drawn from society's lonely, isolated and disadvantaged, individuals from the entire social spectrum were represented. The study also revealed that, though undoubtedly disturbed, most did not have any diagnosable major mental illness. The stalkers in the study by Mullen and colleagues could be grouped into five categories, largely on the basis of the stalker's principal motivation and the context in which the stalking arose. These categories are described below. Their management is discussed in Chapter 5.

The rejected

This is thought to be the largest group of stalkers, comprised predominantly, but not exclusively, of ex-partners. It is therefore not surprising that there is some overlap between the characteristics of this category of stalking and those of domestic violence.

These stalkers respond to an unwelcome end to a close relationship by actions that are intended, at least initially, to achieve reconciliation or retribution. Often their goal may be a fluctuating mixture of both. In most cases the nature of the relationship between stalker and victim is, or was, a sexually intimate one, but it can be any close relationship in which the rejected partner has invested considerable emotional energy. Examples include alliances between close friends, a work partnership, therapists and clients, teachers and students and even family members.

In the most common scenario the rejected partner, usually male, begins stalking his partner after she attempts to end the relationship. The stalker's rage at rejection is often fuelled by distress at the perceived unfairness or humiliation of the rejection. Some stalkers are acutely aware that the lost relationship is in all likelihood irreplaceable. Many concede that a campaign of harassment is unlikely to persuade their ex-partner to return, *but the stalking effectively traps both the victim and perpetrator in a continuing relationship.* For those stalkers who cannot abandon the hope of a reunion the harassment at least preserves some semblance of a connection to the lost partner. Even the activities of those rejected stalkers who are predominantly angry and vengeful are aimed partly at maintaining some sort of relationship.

Few rejected stalkers will have demonstrable psychiatric symptoms, but many will exhibit abnormalities of personality that may amount to full blown *personality disorders.* These are enduring patterns of thinking and behaving which deviate markedly from the individual's culture. They are generally considered to be the product of inborn, biological processes and patterns of behaviour developed in response to life experiences. Personality disorders have their onset in adolescence or early adulthood, if not before. The fourth edition of the American Psychiatric Association's *Diagnostic and Statistical Manual of Mental Disorders* (American Psychiatric Association, 1994) notes that personality disorders lead to clinically significant distress or impairment in the afflicted individual's social, occupational or other important areas of functioning.

There are various types of personality disorders. Those more frequently encountered among rejected stalkers are the *narcissistic* and *dependent* types. The former are characterized by a pervasive pattern of grandiosity, lack of empathy for others and a need for admiration. They often show a sense of entitlement, exploit others to achieve their own ends and may be preoccupied with fantasies of unlimited success, power or ideal love. Excessive dependence is also a common feature of rejected stalkers, often in association with deficient social skills and meagre social networks. Such individuals have frequently invested all their hopes and expectations in the relationship. Some have trouble establishing relationships of any kind, let alone intimate ones. Their reaction to the rejection often has more to do with disbelief and desperation than with shame or rage. They tenaciously cling to the hope that their persistence will be blessed with a reunion.

Paranoid disorders are also not uncommon among the rejected group, excessive jealousy and suspiciousness being common manifestations. These characteristics are often apparent during the relationship and are likely to contribute to its disintegration. The distrustful partners frequently check on the healthy partners' movements, interrogate them and follow and generally harangue them. Assaults are not unusual, as are attacks on the victim's property. After the victim leaves the relationship, the jealous ex-partner asserts his continuing entitlement not just to a relationship but also to the victim's fidelity.

Rejected stalkers may perceive *themselves* as victims. They portray their harassment and intrusions as *provoked* and, consequently, as justified. In addition to traits such as jealousy, possessiveness, clinging dependency and insensitivity to the needs and feelings of others, these individuals may well have a pattern of domestic violence in prior relationships. Often, the current partners are oblivious to their abusive history or learn of it only after they have joined former partners on the stalkers' lists of victims.

Rejected stalkers tend to have the widest repertoire of harassing behaviours. They often follow and approach their victims and repeatedly phone and send letters. They are also more likely than most other groups of stalkers to threaten and even assault their ex-intimates. These can be the most persistent and intrusive of stalkers.

Case example

Trevor and Fiona argued since the day they first met, but the conflict escalated when they moved into an apartment together six months after their relationship began. Around this time, Trevor was made redundant from work and his alcohol consumption increased. During one of their arguments he shoved Fiona against a bookcase, injuring her back. She fled to a girlfriend's apartment and never returned.

Trevor says he was devastated and confused when Fiona walked out. He dismissed the role of his violence and drinking, alleging Fiona was 'screwed in the head' as a consequence of being abused as a child. He argued that 'I'm the best thing that ever happened to that girl' and that she would eventually 'come running back begging'. Nevertheless, he was leaving nothing to chance. He phoned her repeatedly at the homes of her parents and her girlfriend, and when they changed their phone numbers he rang Fiona at work. One night he arrived unannounced and intoxicated at the girlfriend's apartment, hammering loudly on the door and shouting until neighbours contacted the police. Trevor's approaches were generally characterized by pleas for Fiona's return ('If you come back now I'll forgive you'), but his entreaties often became abusive and menacing, especially under the influence of alcohol ('You leave me now, bitch, and your life is *finished*'). Threats were also extended to Fiona's girlfriend for harbouring and 'brainwashing' her and to Fiona's elderly parents.

Fiona ultimately obtained a protective injunction against Trevor. The harassment persisted, with anonymous 'poison pen' faxes to Fiona's work, offal left on her doorstep, graffiti on her girlfriend's driveway and attacks on Fiona's car (acid thrown over the paintwork and a broken windscreen wiper). Trevor continued to leave 'heavy breathing' messages on Fiona's answering machine and she believes that on a few occasions he followed her in his car.

After 15 months of harassment, Trevor's activities finally ended, following his conviction for stalking and a two-month prison sentence. During this time he agreed to accept help for his alcohol and anger problems and to undergo psychiatric counselling. He concedes he did 'just once or twice, out of curiosity' drive past Fiona's home immediately after his release, though, unknown to him, she had since fled interstate.

The intimacy seeker

These stalkers are driven by the need to establish or confirm an intimate relationship with the target. In pursuing this goal, they endow the object of affection with special qualities that make them an ideal partner. His target may be an acquaintance or a complete stranger. Those who stalk the famous ('star stalkers') are generally drawn from either the intimacy seeking group or the incompetent suitors (below).

Intimacy seekers are typically quite persistent in their approaches and communications. They are impervious or oblivious to the victims' negative responses, convinced that their efforts will ultimately be rewarded. These individuals typically share lives bereft of intimacy, often living alone. The fantasized relationship and their love for the victims, together with the accompanying pursuit, offer a solution to their isolation.

Loneliness does not of itself explain the behaviour of intimacy seeking stalkers, however, since most lonely and isolated people presumably do not become stalkers. The other essential ingredient is a *disordered state of mind,* one that enables the individual to create and sustain an attachment to someone who is actively rejecting him. This can be achieved by reinterpreting the negative responses of the victim as encouraging or at least not rejecting. Serious mental disorders are a relatively common finding in this category of stalkers, ranging from severe mental illnesses such as schizophrenia to the personality disorders.

Erotomania

A few intimacy seeking stalkers are convinced their love is reciprocated, irrespective of all evidence to the contrary. Those motivated by a firm but false conviction that they and their victims are *already* in a relationship are considered to be suffering from the illness 'erotomania'. Erotomanic delusions may be the main manifestation of a *delusional disorder,* or they may be secondary to another psychiatric illness (e.g. schizophrenia or mania) or physical condition (e.g. brain damage). Delusional disorder of erotomanic type has also been referred to in the earlier psychiatric literature as *de Clérambault's syndrome* or *psychose passionelle.* Sufferers are often otherwise outwardly normal. Unrestrained by the plausibility of the imagined relationship, erotomanics commonly select people who are physically attractive or of higher social status, or both, but virtually anyone can become the object of an erotomanic's disordered attentions.

Other stalkers in the intimacy seeker category could be regarded as morbidly or pathologically infatuated, but unlike the erotomanic stalkers they are not deluded. An example is John Hinckley Jr, who in 1981 attempted to assassinate President Ronald Reagan. Hinckley had developed an intense and consuming infatuation with the actress Jodie Foster, and after repeated unsuccessful attempts to court her he tried to win her attention by assassinating a public figure. Hinckley was not labouring under any delusion that Foster reciprocated his love, but his infatuation was nonetheless intense and preoccupying and led, through a tortured reasoning process, to a serious attempt on the American president's life.

Intimacy seekers are at least as persistent in their harassment as rejected stalkers, reflecting the importance the fantasized relationship comes to occupy in their lives. Some will pursue their target over several years, tending to favour less immediately intrusive types of communication such as letters and gifts (often in the form of keepsakes and embodiments of love such as flowers and chocolates). Following and surveillance is relatively less common in this group, which may in part reflect the shy, isolated nature of many intimacy seekers.

Declarations of love are the common theme of these stalkers' communications. Rebuffs tend to be ignored or reinterpreted in a more positive light, though occasionally frustration and anger can surface. Aggression, while uncommon, can be directed at a third party who is perceived to be blocking the stalker's access to his beloved. Circumstances in which violence may occur are discussed further in Chapter 4.

Case example

Helen, a nurse, was besotted with a senior staff physician at her hospital. After 'meeting' him on a ward round, for the next six months she hovered around the places he frequented, hoping to glimpse him. A timid 28-year-old, Helen had not spoken a word to the doctor, but she never doubted the depth of his love for her. She 'knew' her feelings were reciprocated because of the way he stroked his moustache in her presence and averted his gaze 'so that others didn't find out about us', the observation that he had changed his car from a convertible two-seater to a 'family' wagon and various other innocent gestures and activities. Helen confessed she knew her imagined paramour was married (and, indeed, had five children), but she protested that the marriage was a 'sham', that she and the doctor were married in a former life and that he had been awaiting her return.

Helen spent increasing amounts of time tailing her imagined lover and observing his home and his family outings. She sent flowers to his home bearing romantic messages which were signed 'Your Helen', distressing the doctor's wife. The barrage of cards and chocolates that ensued did little to ease the woman's suspicions. Indeed, the doctor had in fact strayed, but his actual lover was a medical student. It was the ever present Helen who stumbled upon the lovers fornicating in a secluded part of the hospital. Enraged at the perceived betrayal, she kicked the startled physician in the groin. Helen was ultimately convicted of assault and was ordered to stay away from her victim. She assured the court that she had no intention of 'returning' to a man who had 'cheated' on her.

The incompetent suitor

These are would-be suitors seeking a partner by methods that are unwelcome and counterproductive. Stalkers in this category exhibit varying degrees of impairment in their social functioning and most particularly in their courting skills. They possess a sense of entitlement to a relationship with an individual who has attracted their interest and, like the intimacy seekers, they are impervious to their victims' preferences in the matter. This combination of social ineptitude and entitlement leads to persistent, inappropriate attempts to initiate a relationship with the victim.

This category of stalkers may approximate that of the 'rejected' in size. Though it is likely they exist, in varying degrees of severity, relatively commonly in the community, they are under-represented in the courts and mental health clinics because they stalk for comparatively brief durations and exhibit less overt mental disturbance.

Despite the relative brevity of their harassment, these stalkers tend to have the highest rate of re-offending of all stalker types, repeatedly targeting new victims as they become discouraged by their present quest. They generally prefer direct approaches to their victims rather than communications such as letter writing.

The intimacy seeking and incompetent stalkers share a sense of entitlement to a relationship and a disregard for the real wishes of the victims. However, while the former believe that as a result of true love they have embarked on the most important activity imaginable, the latter simply believe that the object of attention should go out on a date with them. The relationship choices of incompetent suitors and their perceptions of their would-be lover differ little from those of any other aspiring suitor. It is the way in which they seek to establish that relationship that is at odds with the rest of the population. Despite this departure from the norm, few incompetent suitors, as opposed to intimacy seeking stalkers, exhibit major mental illness. They are essentially normal people disabled by poor social skills, self centredness and insensitivity to the needs of others.

Case example

Chris, a 30-year-old draftsman, lived at home with his parents. He had an impoverished social life, confined to just one friend whom he occasionally met for coffee. His long-standing ambition was to find a girlfriend and 'settle down'. His friend (also a single man and the quintessential 'computer nerd') urged Chris to join a dating agency, but these connections never progressed beyond one or two phone calls. He suspected none of these women were functioning at his intellectual level and were intimidated by his sophisticated views on world politics and the financial market. In fact, they found him opinionated and boring.

Chris ultimately found the 'perfect girlfriend', or so he thought, at work. Janet, aged 22, joined the firm as a temporary secretary. Chris quickly noted her 'presentable' appearance, kind nature and willingness to listen to him. She was also single, and a week after her arrival she accepted his invitation to go to the cinema. Janet struggled during the outing to resist his inappropriate efforts to kiss and embrace her. He seemed oblivious to her pleas to 'slow down'. She declined his invitation for coffee after the film, taking a cab home despite his protestations.

Janet expected that Chris would feel foolish upon reflection, and she returned to work with only minor trepidation. To her dismay, Chris seemed more proud than embarrassed, and he appeared to regard her as his girlfriend. She asked him to accompany her to the cafeteria, where, over coffee, she gently explained to him that he was a nice person and interesting company but that she wasn't ready for a relationship at that time. Unfazed, Chris proposed they meet that night for dinner. Janet admits she felt sorry for this man and she was confident he would eventually accept there would be no relationship. She agreed to dinner, during which a tedious and one-sided discussion of his career trajectory evolved into an uncomfortably intimate conversation about marriage and babies.

When Chris next suggested a date, Janet politely but firmly declined. He continued to pester her and to phone her at home, sending her a dozen red roses and a collection of romantic poems on Valentine's Day. Janet left the firm prematurely as a consequence of Chris's persistent advances and the failure of senior personnel to take definitive action. Shortly afterwards the stalking ended. She subsequently learned, however, that Chris was subjecting her attractive replacement to similar harassment.

The resentful

These stalkers are encountered less commonly. They are responding to a perceived insult or injury by stalking activities aimed not just at revenge but also at vindication. Resentful stalkers are motivated primarily by the desire to cause fear and distress in the victim. The victim is often selected because she exemplifies the type of person who oppressed and humiliated the stalker in the past. Indeed, she becomes the embodiment of those against whom the stalker has a multiplicity of grievances. The resentment may generalize beyond a single individual to the entire department, corporation or the 'system'.

Not surprisingly, then, resentful stalkers seldom view their behaviour as victimizing someone more vulnerable than themselves. On the contrary, they perceive *themselves* as the victim striking back against the more powerful forces persecuting them. These stalkers typically experience a gratifying sense of power and control from their harassing behaviours.

Resentful stalking is characteristically a *protracted* campaign of harassment aimed at inducing fear in the perceived oppressor. These individuals often harbour resentment against an unfeeling and rejecting world long before the event that precipitated the stalking. Their resentment becomes channelled into the harassment and focused on the target. Unfortunately, the choice of target frequently appears to the victim and others to be rather arbitrary, ill directed and excessive.

It is perhaps not surprising that stalkers in this group are the most likely to threaten. However, they are among the *least* likely to proceed to an actual assault. This may be explained by the resentful stalker's predominant motivation, which is to create maximum distress to the victim (and, in many instances, other parties) with minimum risk to the stalker.

Case example

Joseph had worked for 32 years in a large government department that was soon to be privatized. He was informed that this would result in the loss of 200 jobs, including his own. Joseph lived alone and had few interests outside his work. His career had always been a source of considerable satisfaction and pride, and he was devastated at the prospect of losing this. He became incensed with the government's sweeping reforms and sent a series of angry letters to his local parliamentary member insisting he reverse the decision that had robbed him of his livelihood. He did not receive a response.

Predictably, Joseph did not cope well with his enforced retirement. He felt it was pointless at the age of 56 to pursue another career. Instead he spent much of his time ruminating and writing letters to his local member of parliament and to newspapers maligning the member and his government. One night he saw the local member of parliament in a television news item attending a glittering state function with his attractive wife. Joseph phoned the politician's private residence and threatened to 'ruin your family's life, the way *you* ruined *mine*'. He felt a sense of triumph when the incident was reported in the newspapers and was consoled by the realization that his oppressors were finally paying for the suffering they had caused. The threatening calls continued.

Joseph's campaign of terror was brought to an abrupt end after a phone trace led to his arrest. The fine he received only aggravated his financial hardship, but he suspended his stalking activities despite his continued hatred for the politicians. He is receiving counselling.

The predatory

Fortunately, these stalkers are relatively rare, probably representing less than 5% of the stalker population. Nonetheless they receive disproportionate exposure in the media and fictional accounts of stalking. The predatory group is comprised almost exclusively of men. His motive is a sexual one, the predatory stalker deriving sexual gratification and control through stalking his victim.

While sexual gratification may be an integral part of the stalking (e.g. the sexually deviant man aroused by repeated obscene phone calls to an unknown woman), the stalking behaviours of this group may be *preparatory* to an assault, usually sexual, upon the victim. Such activities are a combination of information gathering, rehearsal and surreptitious observation. In most cases the stalker's intent is not to disturb or alert the victim before the fantasized or planned attack. This is in contrast to the resentful stalker, who derives gratification through forcing the victim to acknowledge his presence and engendering fear.

Most predatory stalkers have identifiable sexual disorders (known as sexual deviations or *paraphilias*) as well as a criminal record of predominantly sexual offences. Those with *paedophilia* typically target children. The lewd phone caller is said to have *telephonicophilia* (more commonly referred to as *scatologia*).

People in this category have the shortest duration of stalking compared with other groups, and they tend to have the narrowest repertoire of harassment methods. Following and surveillance predominate, though in the case of scatologia telephone calls are the major, if not exclusive, means of intrusion and sexual gratification.

Case example

Andrew had a long history of sexually offensive behaviour. While on parole for the rape of a 14-year-old girl he resumed his previous pattern of cruising past high schools in his car and following teenage schoolgirls. He was particularly drawn to a 13-year-old student and he repeatedly tailed her as she walked home. He twice drove up beside her and offered her a ride, but on each occasion the girl fled. He also secretly photographed his victim and the images were incorporated into his sexual fantasies. When the girl's mother reported Andrew's activities and his car registration number to the police the parolee was promptly apprehended and returned to prison.

Summary

- Stalkers come from all walks of life.
- Most stalkers, around 80%, are male.
- Stalkers do not have a uniform profile, and there is no single motivation for stalking.
- Not all stalkers have frank mental illness.
- Stalkers can be divided into five main types according to their motivation for stalking and the context in which the stalking arises.
- The largest of these groups is the *rejected,* consisting mainly of ex-partners.
- The category of *incompetent suitors* is likely to be more common than originally thought, since they tend not to be as persistent as other stalkers and therefore they are less likely to frequent courts and mental health services.
- *Intimacy seekers* are mentally disturbed and more persistent in their stalking. This category includes the condition *erotomania.*
- *Resentful* stalkers are less common, and *predatory* or sexually motivated stalkers are encountered rarely.

4

Could I be assaulted?

Violence is the most dramatic manifestation of the damage inflicted by stalkers. Instances of violent stalking have been highlighted in recent years in an attempt to impress upon law makers and law enforcers the seriousness of the problem and the need for assertive action. However, violence is by no means the commonest expression of stalking. The conduct of stalkers often evokes distress without them ever laying a hand on their victims. Nonetheless, it is understandable that many stalking victims are concerned for their physical safety. Risk appraisals are also sought by police and the courts and by therapists who treat stalkers or counsel their victims.

Although violence is most commonly directed at the object of attention, other parties may also be attacked, usually because they are perceived as hampering the stalker's pursuit of his victim. Mullen et al. (1999) found that a third of their sample of 145 stalkers attacked their victims, while in 5% of cases violence was directed at others such as the primary victims' families, friends or work colleagues. In most cases the attacks constituted an impulsive lashing out in response to rejection or a perceived insult. The injuries inflicted were largely confined to minor bruises and abrasions.

Research to date has consistently found that it is the *rejected* stalkers who are most prone to assaultive behaviour. In the study by Mullen and co-workers, nearly 60% of the rejected group had attacked their former intimates. Of the six predatory stalkers in this study, half assaulted their victims, in most cases sexually. Violence was less common among the incompetent suitors and the resentful, though a quarter of stalkers in each of these groups attacked their victims. In terms of the pre-existing relationship, ex-intimate victims had a higher risk of being attacked, while those pursued by acquaintances or strangers were at much less risk.

Although in general the rate of violence among intimacy seekers is low, erotomania can occasionally lead to assault. This is typically motivated by jealousy or rage at persistent rejection, and violence is most often directed at the imagined lover. Alternatively, those believed to obstruct the stalker's access to the beloved may be targeted. Erotomanic stalkers who are ultimately violent typically have a history of violence unrelated to their present delusions and stalking activities.

Stalkers can also attack and damage *property*, usually that owned by the victims or involved third parties. In the study by Mullen and colleagues, 40% of stalkers inflicted damage to property, the rejected and resentful groups showing the greatest propensity for this. Victim surveys also reveal that around 10% of stalking victims have had their domestic pets threatened, maimed or killed. The risk factors for property violence are similar to those for personal violence, as detailed below.

Threats by stalkers are more common than actual violence. Over half the stalkers in the study by Mullen and colleagues threatened their victims, and more than a third threatened other parties. The incidence of threats was higher among those with a prior intimate relationship with their victims (the rejected) or those with a real or imagined injury related to a business or professional relationship (the resentful). Intimacy seekers made explicit threats against their fantasized lovers in over 50% of cases.

Less than half of those who threaten will actually put their menacing words into action. Rejected stalkers are the most likely to enact their threats against the victim. The resentful pose the lowest risk of carrying out their threats, preferring terrorism, humiliation and degradation of the victim to the direct use of violence. In less than 20% of cases the stalker is violent without issuing prior threats. Threats should be regarded as promises. Like many promises, not all are fulfilled, but threats in a stalking context should be taken seriously. Threats are themselves acts of violence. They are issued to frighten and intimidate, and for most stalking victims they succeed in those aims.

The presence of a major mental illness in the stalker does not appear to heighten the chances of assaultive behaviour. Indeed, deluded stalkers may pose *less* risk of attack. A notable exception are those with paranoid states, particularly delusional jealousy, which has a sinister reputation for violence directed at the 'unfaithful' partner. The prospect of assault should never be discounted in the paranoid stalker with disordered preoccupations centring on the infidelity of the estranged, imagined or hoped for lover. Those diagnosed with personality disorders and sexual deviations are also more likely to be assaultive.

Substance abuse increases the probability of aggressive behaviour among those with other mental disorders. This association also holds for stalkers. Stalkers who abuse alcohol or drugs, or both, are more likely to threaten, damage property and attack than those who do not. Other robust predictors of violence in offender populations in general, including stalkers, are the nature and extent of prior convictions. Past violent or sexual offences carry the highest risk, but any significant criminal history, almost irrespective of the nature of the offending, increases the probability of assault in the setting of stalking. Past criminal convictions are more frequent among the predatory and rejected groups.

Fortunately, homicidal violence is a rare occurrence with stalkers. There is, however, a tendency for such cases to be widely publicized, provoking understandable alarm amongst victims and the general public. The usual scenario is a rejected stalker who resorts to a final destructive act when he recognizes that his grandiose fantasies of reconciliation will never materialize and that no alternative relationship can suffice.

Pooling of data from existing studies suggests that violent behaviours occur in about a third of stalking cases, but this statistic should be interpreted with caution. These studies have been almost exclusively based on highly selected populations in whom assault might be expected to be over-represented. That is, victim samples have consisted of more severely affected cases and consequently, one could surmise, those at greater risk of having been attacked. When larger, randomly selected community surveys are undertaken these statistics for the prevalence of threats, property damage and personal violence could well prove exaggerated.

On the basis of the available research findings, it is possible to propose a number of factors that are associated with a lower risk of stalker violence. Of course, though reassuring, their presence should not be cause for complacency or the abandonment of personal safety measures.

Stalker features associated with decreased potential for violence

- Female.
- Not in rejected or predatory categories.
- No prior relationship with the victim.
- Absence of severe personality disorder.
- No alcohol or drug problems.
- Compliant with treatment.
- No criminal record.
- Stable employment.
- Adequate social network.
- Absence of threats.

The characteristics of stalkers at high risk of assault can be more confidently advanced, this group attracting the scrutiny of researchers, clinicians and criminal justice experts.

Stalker features associated with an increased potential for violence

- Male.
- Rejected or predatory stalker type.
- Pursuing an ex-intimate.
- Severe personality disorder.
- Alcohol or drug abuse, or both.
- Poor compliance with treatment.
- Criminal record, especially for sexual and violent offences.
- Unemployed.
- Socially isolated.
- Issues threats.
- High levels of anger directed at the victim.
- Strong sense of entitlement.
- Fantasizes about an assault.
- Plans an attack.
- An affinity with violence (this includes an interest in, and access to, firearms).

In their management of stalkers it is essential for therapists to identify those with a significant probability of proceeding to assault and to intervene to prevent that progression. This occurs, however, in a context of overcoming the *totality* of stalking behaviours. As already noted, violence is not an essential ingredient in the stalking victim's recipe for suffering and upheaval. Stalking is in itself a form of violence.

Summary

- Violence occurs in a minority of stalking cases, though certain types of stalker, such as the rejected and the predatory, are more likely than others to assault their target.
- Life threatening violence is rare.
- Attacks may also be made on third parties, such as the victim's family.
- Most of those who threaten do not proceed to violence against person or property.
- In less than 20% of cases the stalker is violent without issuing prior threats.
- Rejected and resentful stalkers are the groups most likely to threaten their victims.
- The rejected are the group most likely to carry out their threats, while the resentful have a substantially lower risk of acting on their threats.
- In general, stalkers with a major mental illness are less prone to violence. However, stalkers with pathological jealousy pose a greater risk to their victim.
- Other factors that increase the stalker's likelihood of violent behaviour and threats include abuse of drugs or alcohol, or both, and a prior criminal record.

5

Can stalkers be treated?

Many stalkers are treatable. This is particularly so for those whose actions are a manifestation of mental illness for which standard treatments are available. But even in the absence of major psychiatric symptoms stalkers may exhibit modifiable abnormalities of personality and social functioning. The dilemma is usually bringing stalkers to treatment because most dispute their mental instability or even that they are stalking, and few are keen to relinquish their activities.

It may be of little comfort to victims to hear that many stalkers are tormented individuals. This is not intended to excuse the stalker for his actions or to elicit sympathy. It nonetheless provides some rationale for treating stalkers and explains why remedies based on punishment alone often fall short of the mark. Stalking is a criminal behaviour, but the most effective approach to its eradication typically combines both legal sanctions and psychiatric interventions in varying ratios. Incarceration is unlikely to achieve a long-term resolution of the problem, although it can play a legitimate part in granting the victim some reprieve and protection from serious harm.

Stalkers seldom present themselves for psychiatric treatment, and even then their motivations may be suspicious. Some, for example, will appear to co-operate with mental health services in an attempt to manipulate the outcome of an impending court case. Only a relatively small number of stalkers fulfil the criteria for civil commitment (i.e. admission to a psychiatric hospital as an involuntary patient) under mental health legislation. Thus, in all but a few cases stalkers cannot be committed to psychiatric hospitals for treatment. Those that are will not necessarily remain in hospital for extended periods given the pressures upon our overburdened mental health system. In practice, criminal proceedings may be one of the few means by which stalkers can be brought to the attention of appropriate treatment services.

At present, treatment is not given due consideration within the criminal justice system. Protective injunctions, fines, suspended sentences and peace bonds (also known as good behaviour bonds or bind overs to keep the peace) punish the conduct but generally lack provisions to ensure the stalker is psychiatrically assessed. Community dispositions such as probation and community based orders are preferable. With these, magistrates can attach conditions, in particular that the defendant complies with psychiatric assessment and treatment. These orders need to be of sufficient duration to initiate referral to the relevant mental health facility and to engage the offender in treatment. Often, stalkers who can be persuaded to acknowledge the personal damage and losses inherent in their behaviour will elect to continue therapy voluntarily, even after their statutory order has expired. Stalking victims should communicate these options to the police and prosecuting authorities (see Chapter 10).

Managing stalkers by type

The rejected

Stalkers in this category are seldom so disturbed and disordered that they cannot calculate their own advantage. Though seemingly dedicated stalkers, when the price for the continued pursuit of their ex-intimates exceeds a certain threshold many will abandon their quests. This threshold may in some cases be the mere threat of civil action. For others, particularly those with a history of court appearances, it may constitute a suspended or actual term of imprisonment.

This does not mean there is no role for therapeutic interventions in this group. Relapses of further stalking activities may well be diminished if not prevented by focused counselling and support. Although there are no magical treatments for disordered personalities, various psychological therapies can prove useful. These stalkers are often angry, distressed individuals, the loss of the relationship having left them adrift without alternative social supports or even occasional contacts. They require help to let go and to grieve appropriately the loss of their former intimates. Counselling can improve their social skills and help them develop new social outlets and ultimately form less troubled relationships. For those with a major mental illness such as a paranoid disorder, delusional jealousy or depression, definitive psychiatric treatment is often effective in alleviating the stalker's distress and, by ending the stalking, that of the victim.

Unfortunately, as earlier noted, most stalkers are not willing participants in treatment and the rejected subgroup are certainly no exception. While in some instances the mental health system can compel them to receive treatment this usually applies to only a relatively small proportion of stalkers with frank mental illness that immediately endangers the stalker's life or that of another person. Few rejected stalkers will satisfy all these criteria, so that bringing them to therapy more often becomes the responsibility of concerned family and friends or the judicial system.

The intimacy seeker

Treating the mental disorder that underlies the stalking is the most effective approach in this group. Legal sanctions alone rarely deter intimacy seekers, because they typically regard such measures as challenges to be overcome. Even imprisonment may be perceived as a test of devotion rather than punishment.

Case example

Lisa, a single 35-year-old woman, was referred by the court for psychiatric evaluation. She had been pursuing a champion golfer over a two-year period, insisting that they were secretly married. She repeatedly approached her imagined spouse at golf tournaments and public functions and even broke into his home on one occasion to cook him a meal. Lisa was not in the least discouraged by repeated police warnings. She contended that the police were actually security guards *disguised* as police, deployed by her 'husband' to protect her from the media attention that she would inevitably attract as a celebrity sportsman's wife.

Lisa was diagnosed with erotomania. This did not appear to be secondary to any other major mental illness since, apart from her delusions of being loved by this famous man, her mental functioning was unimpaired. Although Lisa had little insight into her illness and therefore her need for treatment, she agreed to commence antipsychotic medication, perceiving this as the 'price one pays for true love'. Her delusions abated over subsequent weeks and she ceased her stalking activities, removed the 'wedding' ring she had previously worn with pride and announced that she didn't think she could face a life of 'living out of suitcases in the media eye'.

Subsequently, unknown to her psychiatrist, Lisa discontinued her tablets for several months, during which time she drove past the golfer's home on a few occasions and purchased tickets to a golf tournament. Fortunately, the re-emergence of erotomanic delusions was detected early and treatment was reinstituted. She has since complied with treatment and her psychotic beliefs have not returned.

The incompetent suitor

This group responds relatively well to judicial sanctions supplemented with counselling. However, the challenge is to prevent them from reverting to stalking when next their attention is captured by what they perceive to be other eligible partners. Counselling focuses on improving social skills and instilling empathy and consideration for others, but this is seldom an easy feat. As is often the case, the closer one is to the norm psychologically and behaviourally the more difficult it can be for mental health professionals to assist in that change.

The resentful

This group is more difficult than others to engage in treatment. Again, most resentful stalkers do not have major mental illness, but paranoid personalities are common. Like their rejected counterparts they can usually calculate their own advantage. Confronted with criminal sanctions many will withdraw from stalking, although this is more likely to succeed in the relatively early stages before the harassment has become firmly entrenched. By then, resentful stalkers have often invested so much of themselves, persuaded as they are of the justice and righteousness of their actions, that withdrawal without total loss of face has become virtually impossible. Mental illnesses, in particular paranoid delusions, are more often diagnosed in this resistant subgroup. Legal sanctions, even terms of imprisonment, are unlikely to impact on their behaviour and may only reinforce their feelings of persecution. In these cases psychiatric treatment is crucial to ending the stalking.

The predatory

The most effective means of ending sexually motivated stalking involves treatment of the underlying sexual deviation. Treatment programmes for sexual offenders are now available in many centres. These employ psychological techniques aimed at abolishing deviant sexual arousal patterns and providing offenders with skills and strategies to prevent future relapses.

Often these individuals, like sexual offenders in general, deny that they have a problem and reject therapeutic interventions. Hence, adequate treatment can seldom be delivered in the absence of legal sanctions that mandate their participation in a treatment programme. Some offenders who pose an unacceptable risk to their victims or the wider community will be imprisoned. They can participate in prison sex offender treatment programmes where these exist, and treatment in the community is often provided after their release, usually as a condition of their parole order.

Summary

- Many stalkers are treatable, but the *delivery* of treatment is often hampered by their poor compliance.
- Few stalkers meet statutory criteria for involuntary commitment to a psychiatric facility.
- The most effective approach to the eradication of stalking is the appropriate combination of legal sanctions and psychiatric interventions.
- Magistrates can mandate psychiatric treatment by making this a condition of any noncustodial (community) sentence.
- Most rejected stalkers eventually respond to legal sanctions. Counselling can help them to grieve the loss of their former partner and improve their social adjustment.
- Intimacy seekers respond best to treatment of the underlying psychiatric condition.
- Incompetent suitors generally respond to criminal sanctions, together with counselling aimed at improving social competence.
- Some resentful stalkers respond to legal penalties, while others whose behaviour is more entrenched or who exhibit frank mental illness will require psychiatric treatment.
- Predatory stalkers respond best to legal sanctions and specialist treatment of their sexual deviation.

6

Who are the victims of stalking?

Although we may take comfort from the observation that relatively few people in our society will have their lives invaded by a stalker, as noted in Chapter 2 the experience of being stalked is by no means rare. No one can claim immunity from a stalker's attentions by virtue of age, gender, social class, occupation, religion or cultural background. In large community samples a fifth of all stalking victims were male, and stalkers may pursue individuals of their own gender (Pathé et al., 2000).

Victims fall into six broad groups, based on the nature of the prior relationship between victim and stalker and the context in which the stalking arises.

Previous partners

Most stalking victims belong to this category, a typical example being a woman who previously shared an intimate relationship with her (usually) male stalker. For some victims, harassment begins before the relationship ends, their partners being increasingly intrusive, controlling and jealous. They may be subjected to following by their partner, unwanted approaches at their workplace, property damage, even assaults. This intimidation and control often serve to isolate the victim from outside support, hindering her prospect of leaving the relationship.

Victims in this category are exposed to the widest range of harassment methods. Persistent following, repeated phone calls, threats and assaults are more likely to be reported by this group. Their stalkers are more persistent than most, though they may also prove more amenable than many others to legal sanctions. The most tenacious and unyielding tend to be cases in which the victim and stalker share children, especially where the stalker has legitimate visiting rights, and where the stalker is pathologically jealous, a disorder requiring psychiatric intervention.

Where the romantic liaison has been relatively brief ('date' stalkers) violence is less characteristic, the stalker having a relatively smaller emotional investment in the relationship. Often the victim ends the liaison because the partner's behaviour is odd or discomforting. The importance of making an assertive exit from these situations, regardless of the partner's anger or his attempts to evoke sympathy or guilt in the victim, is discussed in Chapter 8.

Guilt is common among victims in this category. Some blame themselves for their choice of partner, and this may be reinforced by admonishments from family and friends, whose wisdom owes much to hindsight. Professional sources of 'help' can be equally judgemental. In the vast majority of cases, however, prospective stalkers have no flashing lights or warnings tattooed on their foreheads to alert would-be partners. Most do not look disturbed, often presenting as intelligent and even charismatic individuals. These victims can suffer substantial harassment and their needs are in no way diminished by any intimacy they may once have shared with their stalkers.

Casual acquaintances and friends

These victims may have had a casual social encounter with the stalker, who is usually an intimacy seeker or incompetent suitor. Another scenario is the victim who becomes embroiled in a dispute with a neighbour, who then proceeds to stalk her. The harassing neighbour often fits the profile of the resentful stalker.

Case example

Pam and Craig were happy in their home in the suburbs until Tom, an elderly bachelor, moved in next door. He was an irascible and suspicious recluse who rejected their attempts to be neighbourly. A seemingly minor dispute over fence repairs – Tom believing he had been overcharged by Craig – escalated into a veritable war that remained confined to the neighbourhood setting. Tom was convinced, in the absence of any evidence, that the couple were 'drug dealers' and that they ran an illegal brothel at home. He reported these activities to the police on countless occasions, but their investigations failed to expose anything untoward and they ceased to respond to his calls.

Tom surrounded his home with an elaborate assortment of booby traps to keep the neighbours from trespassing. He frequently intruded on *their* property, however, depositing newspaper cuttings (mostly stories relating to drug crimes) on their doorstep. He repeatedly uprooted Pam's plants, believing them to be drug crops. He once adorned the front of their house with a banner saying 'WHOREHOUSE'. He sat in his kitchen at night, binoculars and camera at the ready, watching for activity in the next-door bedroom. He photographed Craig and Pam's visitors (convinced they were clients or junkies). He paid a schoolboy to conduct a letter box drop in the immediate neighbourhood anonymously warning others of the evil in their midst and inciting them to take action against the couple.

Fortunately, Tom's allegations had little credibility amongst the neighbours, who had known Craig and Pam for many years. Although Tom was generally viewed as a 'paranoid, demented old man' the objects of his resentment were well and truly at the end of their tether. Police cautions had minimal impact on Tom's harassing behaviours, any dispute resolution process seemed doomed to fail and a protective injunction would similarly prove difficult to enforce as long as they continued to live in close proximity to the harassing party. After considerable debate and police advice they moved to another suburb. Tom made no attempt to pursue them, having achieved his aim to evict them.

Professional contacts

Health care providers, especially psychiatrists, psychologists, social workers and general practitioners, are particularly vulnerable to stalking. So, too, are teachers and lawyers. The patients and clients who harass them are most often categorized as intimacy seekers, incompetent suitors or resentful stalkers, though the termination of a therapeutic relationship may give rise to rejected stalking patterns.

Almost any professional who comes into contact with isolated and disordered people and in whom sympathy and attention is easily reconfigured as romantic interest may be vulnerable. Psychiatrist Dr Doreen Orion gives a poignant account of stalking by a former female patient with erotomania (see *I Know You Really Love Me* in the reading guide).

This is no doubt an under-reported phenomenon, some professionals being inhibited by fears of being blamed or disbelieved. While violence is fortunately uncommon, the preferred methods of harassment being phone calls, letters and gifts, these victims nonetheless report distress, disruption and disillusionment with their chosen profession.

Case example

Teresa, a 37-year-old general practitioner, was working in the country when she first met her stalker. Forty-year-old Vince presented with minor 'flu symptoms and requested a medical certificate. He expressed his delight that he would be seen by Teresa and not by her 60-year-old male colleague, for whom she was doing a six month locum. He made several discomforting and inappropriate comments about Teresa's physical appearance and probed her for personal details such as where she was living and with whom. Teresa politely discouraged his overfamiliarity, but she found it difficult to end the consultation because he wanted to talk about his loneliness and 'depression', the stressors in his life and his thoughts of suicide. Teresa listened sympathetically and arranged for him to see a counsellor.

The next day Teresa was greeted at work by a large bouquet of flowers, with the accompanying message *'to the new doc with the beautiful brown eyes'*, signed by Vince. Although she again felt uneasy, she took comfort in the expectation that he would be seeing the counsellor and the infatuation would pass. However, Vince never pursued the referral. He instead arrived at the medical practice up to a dozen times a week, with various minor complaints. He also brought more flowers and gifts of confectionery 'for the secretary'. As the sole practitioner, Teresa initially felt obliged to see Vince but eventually confronted him. She made it patently clear that a relationship was not a consideration and that she would be leaving within a few months. He claimed he understood and would not pester her further at the clinic, but instead he turned up at her home. He offered to help Teresa around the garden ('It must be hard not having a man about'). She insisted she did not want him around so he waited in his car outside her house and sounded his horn whenever she arrived home, claiming he was 'just making sure she got home safely'.

Teresa was reluctant to involve the police because Vince was a patient and he had confided that he had suicidal tendencies, but she felt threatened by his intrusions and especially his apparent inability to accept the purely professional nature of their relationship. The police warned Vince to stay away from the doctor, threatening to charge him with stalking. Vince heeded the caution and the last weeks of Teresa's locum were tense but uneventful.

Workplace contacts

Stalking that arises in a work related context is typically perpetrated by co-workers, though up to a third of cases involve clients or customers. Resentment is a common motivation, but victims of workplace stalking may also be pursued by intimacy seekers or incompetent suitors. Of course, it is not unusual for rejected stalkers to extend their harassment to their ex-partner's place of employment, repeatedly telephoning and following the victim to work, arriving unannounced or loitering outside.

Some workers may become the focus of a resentful stalker's embitterment and vengeance following organizational changes or disciplinary action. The stalker may believe that he has been unfairly passed over in favour of the victim and may contest the perceived discrimination before various tribunals and appeal boards, with escalating harassment as the complaints are dismissed. The victim in these circumstances may be subject to threats, and she may find her activities and performance being monitored by the aggrieved worker, who may even maintain a dossier on her. Approaches to the management of workplace stalking are discussed in Chapter 9.

Strangers

Victims in this category have had no prior contact with their stalkers or are not aware of any. Usually, stalkers who target strangers fall into the intimacy seeking or incompetent groups. The victim may be chosen by virtue of her elevated social status or physical attractiveness, though this is by no means always the case. Indeed, those victims who have attempted to downplay their assets have not necessarily dampened their stalkers' enthusiasm.

Predatory stalkers not uncommonly target unknown victims, who are usually women, but men and children can also be victimized in accordance with the stalker's sexual preferences. These victims may be unaware of their stalkers' attention, the duration of pursuit in most cases being relatively brief.

The famous

These victims are most often encountered through radio, television and film but may also include politicians, royalty, sports stars and other prominent public figures. Some celebrities attract multiple pursuers, either serially or concurrently. Their stalkers are predominantly drawn from the incompetent, the intimacy seekers and the resentful.

Secondary victims

In addition to primary victims (that is, the person primarily targeted by the stalker), a number of other individuals may become the indirect or secondary victims of a stalker. A common target is the victim's current partner, who may be seen by the intimacy seeking or incompetent stalker particularly as competition. In these circumstances the secondary victim may conceivably be at greater risk of attack than the *primary* victim. Similarly, the rejected stalker may be outraged when his victim forms another relationship, and the new partner can become the predominant focus for the stalker's rage. (In practice, this is not a common scenario because few people who are actively being stalked have the time, energy, self confidence or trust in others to establish new relationships, and many are loathe to expose an innocent person to their private hell).

Family and friends of the victim may attract a stalker's wrath and they can become the target of harassment because they are viewed (often correctly) as shielding the victim, or 'brainwashing' the victim against them. Resentful and rejected stalkers may threaten family members to torment the primary victims, children not infrequently becoming the targets of these threats.

Case example

After Maria ended her relationship with her boyfriend of 18 months he refused to leave her alone. He phoned her up to 60 times a day and frequently called at the home she shared with her parents and brother. He begged her to reconsider, offering her 'marriage and lots of babies', but on some occasions he arrived intoxicated and was verbally abusive. Maria's family were extremely protective, refusing to allow him any contact with her. He berated and threatened them, stabbing the tyres on the brother's car and shattering the mother's pot plants. Then, after returning one day from an outing in the park with her two-year-old niece, Maria received an anonymous call – undoubtedly her stalker – threatening to harm the child.

Work colleagues may unwittingly become secondary victims. Again, they may be perceived as thwarting the stalker's efforts to access the victim, e.g. when they refuse to bring the victim to the phone or to allow the stalker entry to the work premises.

There is a range of other parties who find themselves the innocent secondary focus of a stalker's attentions, including the housemates and boarders of stalking victims. As noted for new partners, victims often feel guilty for the trouble they have 'caused' others. This is in some instances reinforced by the initial response of secondary victims, whose own fear and helplessness may prompt angry recriminations. Of course, the primary target is no more responsible for the harassment of others than for her own harassment. Nonetheless, it is important for stalking victims to be alert to the dangers to which their associates are exposed and to ensure all potential victims are informed of the stalkers' activities. They, like the stalker's primary focus, need to be properly prepared and to have established an adequate safety plan.

Summary

- Virtually anyone can be stalked.
- Approximately one fifth of stalking victims are male.
- Women can be stalked by women and men can be stalked by men, regardless of the victim's sexual orientation.
- Most victims are stalked by a previous partner.
- Members of virtually any profession that casts them in the role of helper to the lonely and disordered may be vulnerable to stalking, especially teachers, lawyers and health professionals.
- Stalking that arises in the workplace is typically motivated by resentment, but workplace stalkers may also be intimacy seekers or incompetent suitors. The victim's workplace is often part of the rejected stalker's expansive territory.
- Stalkers who target strangers are usually intimacy seekers or incompetent suitors.
- Celebrity victims are most often targeted by intimacy seeking, incompetent and resentful stalkers.
- Some individuals may become indirect, or secondary, victims of stalking.

7

The impact of stalking

Unlike many other criminal offences, stalking is characterized by its repetition and persistence. The stalking victim is usually exposed to multiple forms of harassment, often involving threatening and traumatic incidents that are experienced as unpredictable and beyond the victim's control.

Research into the psychological effects of traumatic experiences such as natural disasters, war and sexual assault suggests that stress related symptoms develop more commonly in situations where the individual feels inescapably under threat over a *protracted period*, as occurs in stalking. *Unpredictability* is another important factor contributing to significant levels of stress. This is prominent in stalking situations, victims commonly experiencing a proliferation of uncertainties as the stalking progresses. Events involving a *loss of control* also appear to generate more persistent disquiet than circumstances where control could never be expected, as in the case of natural disasters. A stalking victim's feelings of helplessness can be reinforced by an unresponsive or ineffectual justice system. Often, their assumptions of living in a fair and safe society are shattered.

Trauma research has also looked at factors that *protect* victims from the development of disabling symptoms. Social support plays a central part, yet this is sometimes compromised in stalking victims. Stalking typically produces in the victim high levels of arousal and a pervasive distrust in others. Although such suspicion and caution may be entirely appropriate, they can also alienate victims from their usual sources of support, leading to social isolation. Even the most robust of friendships and more intimate relationships can be sorely tested by the persistent intrusions of a stalker and the manner in which the victim responds to the harassment. Other factors may combine to isolate the victim further, including deterioration in work performance, leading in some cases to withdrawal from the workforce.

Studies of the impact of stalking on its victims have relied on samples of people who are likely to belong to the more severely affected end of the range of victims. Nevertheless, these surveys highlight the substantial distress and disruption wrought by this crime and the far reaching nature of this damage. The findings will be summarized here, but for a more detailed discussion see Pathé and Mullen (1997), and Doris M Hall's chapter in Meloy (1998) in the reading guide.

Nearly all victims of stalking in surveys and (not surprisingly) those referred for counselling report that stalking has had a deleterious impact on their psychological, social and/or occupational functioning. Indeed, over 90% of the 100 Australian victims surveyed by Pathé and Mullen were forced to make substantial lifestyle changes in response to being stalked. Common examples included avoidance of certain locations where the stalker might be, installing additional security measures, obtaining unlisted telephone numbers and restricting social outings. Some victims had resorted to extreme and often costly measures to evade their stalker, with varying success, such as changing their motor vehicle, their home and even their name.

Over half of the Australian sample felt compelled to reduce or cease work or school attendance. This was usually a response to the stalker's repeated attempts to contact the victim at her workplace or en route to work or home, but some victims were unable to work as a consequence of stress symptoms. Appointments with doctors and counsellors and attendances at court (e.g. to obtain protection orders) contributed to high rates of absenteeism. A third of this sample ultimately felt compelled to change their workplace, school or career. A few victims were fired by employers who were either unsympathetic or who felt threatened by the stalker's repeated intrusions at the workplace.

Most people who have been subjected to significant levels of stalking experience adverse effects on their physical or mental wellbeing, or both. Commonly reported symptoms include feelings of powerlessness, helpless- ness and violation, aggressive thoughts towards the perpetrator, guilt (however misplaced), anxiety (most often manifest as 'jumpiness', 'shakes', panic attacks and hyperalertness), poor concentration, impaired appetite, sleep disturbance, weight loss (or weight gain), weakness, fatigue, lack of motivation, nausea, altered bowel habit and headaches. Some victims feel they have undergone a personality change, becoming less friendly and outgoing and more introverted, cautious, irritable and 'paranoid'. Many feel suspicious of others' motives. Suicidal thoughts were reported by a quarter of Pathé and Mullen's sample, some believing that this would be their only escape from a life sentence of stalking.

Symptoms related to trauma are common among victims of stalking. These are anxiety and avoidance symptoms that emerge following exposure to major trauma. The psychiatric disorder most directly related to trauma is post-traumatic stress disorder (PTSD). In the fourth edition of the American Psychiatric Association's *Diagnostic and Statistical Manual of Mental Disorders* (DSM-IV) (American Psychiatric Association, 1994) PTSD is classified as one of the anxiety disorders. DSM-IV groups the symptoms of PTSD into three clusters:

- Re-experiencing of the traumatic event or events through intense and intrusive thoughts, images, perceptions or dreams. Stalking victims not infrequently report vivid recollections or flashbacks of the stalking that are recurrent and distressing, often triggered by everyday occurrences. These may include the ringing of the phone or glimpsing the particular model and colour of car driven by the stalker.
- Excessive arousal, resulting in difficulty falling or staying asleep, hypervigilance (excessive watchfulness for signs of danger), difficulty concentrating, irritability or outbursts of anger and an exaggerated startle response or jumpiness. These are quite common in stalking victims, either alone or in combination with the other features making up a diagnosis of PTSD.
- Persistent and deliberate avoidance of stimuli associated with or resembling the trauma. Numbing of general responsiveness is in a sense the mind's way of shutting out overwhelming stimulation. Symptoms include feelings of detachment or estrangement from others or a sense of a foreshortened future.

Case example

Wendy lived alone when the harassment began. It started with a series of obscene phone calls from an anonymous man. The content of these suggested the caller had been monitoring her movements because he described the car she drove, the places she visited and the outfits she was wearing. Then her underwear disappeared from her clothesline overnight, the underpants later returned in the mail with the crotches cut out. Wendy was alarmed. The police had been notified after the first few phone calls but their investigation had so far revealed little, and she was growing increasingly impatient and fearful. She no longer had the confidence to leave her apartment and was experiencing extreme anxiety and frequent panic attacks. At these times she felt overwhelmed, engulfed in fear, lightheaded, clammy and unable to breathe properly. Her fingers tingled (a consequence of hyperventilation) and she thought she must be losing her mind.

Wendy moved back to her parents' home, but her anxiety levels remained high and she refused to go out or to see anyone. She was afraid to fall asleep because of repeated vivid nightmares in which her faceless persecutor chased and attacked her with scissors. At times she cried but mostly she felt nothing, 'like an empty, numb, nothingness inside'. Wendy jumped whenever the phone rang, a reaction that persisted long after her stalker was apprehended. She also felt unbearably anxious when the mail arrived, and she could no longer bring herself to do the laundry. She discarded all the underwear she owned at that time and, although her detachment from others eventually receded, she remained cautious in her relationships with men.

High levels of anxiety and associated discomfort lead some sufferers to treat themselves with tranquillizers (e.g. diazepam (Valium) or alprazolam (Xanax)) and/or alcohol. While these substances may provide some temporary relief there is significant potential for chemical dependence, compounding the victim's problems. Indiscriminate use of sedatives and sleeping tablets may also place the victim at risk of accidents and impair her capacity to defend herself. Victims who increase their cigarette consumption in response to stalking further endanger their health. Physical symptoms and the development or aggravation of various illnesses such as peptic ulcers, skin conditions, asthma, hypertension and nervous tics have all been observed in chronically stressed victims of stalking.

Research suggests that stalking victims at greatest risk of developing stress related symptoms are those who report being *followed* or exposed to *violence.* Victims who have had a prior intimate relationship with their stalkers (whom we know to be at greater risk of violence) more commonly develop stress related symptoms. Being female also increases vulnerability to traumatic stress symptoms.

While a substantial number of stalking victims experience many of the symptoms of PTSD, significantly fewer will qualify for a diagnosis of this disorder. This is because the DSM-IV requires that 'the person experienced, witnessed, or was confronted with an event or events that involved *actual or threatened death or serious injury, or a threat to the physical integrity of self or others;* the person's response involved intense fear, helplessness, or horror' (American Psychiatric Association 1994, p 424, italics added). As discussed earlier, actual or threatened physical injury is not a universal feature in stalking cases. However, we know that *physical* violence is certainly not a prerequisite for the emergence of significant levels of distress and disability among stalking victims. Victims commonly report chronic fear in the absence of any physical assault or even explicit threats. They ascribe their suffering to the constant *menace* and persistent, unpredictable and often incomprehensible nature of the stalkers' intrusions. Some even admit that being attacked by the stalker would be a *relief* from the secretive and intangible activities of their tormentor; physical assault might at least be more readily recognized by the authorities and treated as a legitimate law enforcement issue.

Psychological and physical problems are common but not inevitable consequences of being stalked. When they do occur, however, they may have a considerable impact on the victim's life and may require professional intervention. While ending the stalking is of course crucial to the restoration of the victim's wellbeing, stress related symptoms do not necessarily subside immediately. Some, such as mistrust and hypervigilance, may persist for a period of time, though not necessarily at maladaptive or disabling levels. The management of these symptoms is discussed in Chapter 12.

Summary

- Stalking commonly, but not inevitably, has a deleterious impact on the psychological, social and/or occupational functioning of its victims.
- Dependence on tranquillizers is a real risk in stalking victims, as is increased cigarette and alcohol consumption. Stress and self treatment with these substances can endanger the victim's physical health.
- Stalking victims are vulnerable to the development of trauma related stress symptoms because these occur more commonly in situations of protracted threat and where the trauma is perceived as inescapable, unpredictable and beyond the victims' control.

- Stalking victims who may be at greatest risk of developing traumatic stress symptoms are ex-intimates, those exposed to physical violence and those subjected to following.
- Social support plays a central part in protecting victims from the disabling affects of traumatic stress symptoms.
- The psychological impact of stalking may necessitate professional intervention.
- For some victims, recovery may be slow and certain symptoms, such as watchfulness, may persist.

8

Reducing your chances of victimization

Clearly, the best means of escaping harm at the hands of a stalker is to avoid succumbing to his advances in the first place. Those already snarled in the stalkers' nets often ask if there is anything they could or should have done differently. While it may allay their guilt and self blame to know that in many cases little could have been done to avoid their stalkers' attentions, it doubtless offers meagre comfort to those grappling with feelings of powerlessness and teetering on the margins of an increasingly malevolent world. In fact, there are certain characteristics in any would-be suitor that signal potential to be a stalker. This chapter outlines a number of measures aimed at reducing the likelihood of ever becoming a victim of stalking, while the following chapter will provide current victims with strategies for deterring their stalkers and halting the progression to long-term harassment.

Identifying the would-be stalker

Stalkers seldom have any distinguishing features that could forewarn potential prey. Few will volunteer any criminal history, and those who do are likely to deny or minimize the seriousness of their offending. Problems in previous relationships are commonly rationalized, with the previous partner depicted as the dysfunctional party. In some instances, the stalker will continue to harass a former intimate even while embarking on another relationship.

There is generally little that can be done to prevent victimization by a stranger. However, when there has been a previous relationship, be it intimate, work related, professional or casual in nature, certain features dictate a need for caution. These include:
- possessiveness and excessive jealousy,
- highly manipulative behaviour,

- exerts an unreasonable amount of control in the relationship (e.g. dictating partner's friends, wardrobe, even her diet),
- demanding unrealistic levels of commitment at an early stage of the relationship,
- moods that oscillate between the extremes of undying devotion and angry rejection,
- poor frustration tolerance,
- abusiveness in the relationship,
- hypersensitivity,
- excessive dependence,
- insecurity and low self esteem,
- obsessive characteristics (e.g. an all consuming passion for a celebrity),
- no close friends.

Though hardly specific indicators, such characteristics should sound alarm bells. Trust your instincts. The longer you tolerate this relationship the more difficulties you are likely to encounter when it ends.

Finally, *never date a person out of pity* and certainly do not date somebody who threatens to commit suicide if you will not see him. In doing so you will surely be courting a stalker.

Declining and ending relationships

Most individuals confronted with the unwanted advances of would-be suitors or estranged intimates feel ill equipped to counter them. Even those who are customarily assertive can be inhibited by sensitivity to the other's feelings (despite the callous disregard that is being shown for theirs) or by fears of a hostile reaction. However, vague and unassertive responses increase the likelihood of misinterpretation and manipulation by the stalker. Bear in mind that a substantial proportion of stalkers are socially incompetent and will fail to grasp obvious, let alone subtle, social cues.

If you do not want a relationship it is important to convey this message in plain, unambiguous terms. A succinct example is 'I do not want a relationship with you'. The individual's wishes are unequivocal; no additional explanation is necessary. *Do not engage in any further discussions with the pursuer or indulge him in counter argument or negotiation.* You are not obliged to provide explanations for your decisions to anyone, particularly when he has persisted in unwelcome behaviour. Indeed, supplying explanations often gives the pursuer the opportunity to challenge your decision. Statements such as 'I'm sorry, but I'm not interested in a relationship at present' or 'I'm too busy right now' may imply that you could be interested in a relationship some time in the future. Worse, 'I already have a boyfriend' may be interpreted as 'I'd go out with you but for my boyfriend'. This may place your partner or any other close friend perceived to be your boyfriend (or girlfriend) at risk from your pursuer, who will regard him as the only obstacle to having a relationship with you.

Your wishes should be stated firmly and reasonably, in a manner that allows the person to retain some dignity. Where possible it is important to avoid giving him further reasons, particularly resentment and anger, to harass you. You must avoid letting him down gently by delivering your message in instalments. This is not doing him any favours, and it serves only to prolong the relationship from which you are trying to extricate yourself. It may also signal that you are undecided or ambivalent about what you want and instil hope that the pursuer's persistence will eventually be rewarded.

You should try to deliver the message in person and directly to him, in a public place or other venue where you feel safe. Using a go-between such as a family member often fails because the pursuer interprets this as the *family's* wishes, not yours. Conveying your position by phone or letter may give him the opportunity to protest that he did not receive or understand the message. In some circumstances, however, such as when the individual is known to have a history of violence or to have behaved in a threatening manner, it is inadvisable to deliver the message in person. In such situations, seek the advice of police and at the very least ensure any meeting occurs in the company of others.

When your wishes are conveyed by these means a *reasonable* person, however disappointed, will ultimately respect your decision and withdraw. Deliberate disregard for your wishes and persistence in unwanted contact only confirm the wisdom of your decision to terminate or decline contact with this individual. Stalking should never be regarded as a normal or acceptable form of behaviour when a relationship ends.

Protecting personal information

- Keep as much information as possible out of public records. Be selective about disclosing you personal details. Limit the distribution of your home address and phone numbers to trusted service providers. Assume that any information you give out to the commercial sector will not be held in confidence.
- Remove your home address from business cards and personal cheques.
- With the recent introduction in Australia of a goods and services tax it is compulsory for agencies and businesses to register for an Australian Business Number. Registrants should be aware that their personal details including address, telephone numbers and date of birth are accessible on the Internet through the Department of Fair Trading's website.
- Where possible, provide a business or post office box address in those situations where you are asked to disclose contact details.
- Consider renting a post office box address for correspondence. This will also circumvent the theft of confidential mail from a private letter box.
- When advising businesses of your new mail box address, request that they delete your old address from their records.
- Those who do not have a post office box should at least install a secure or lockable mail box, so that others cannot intercept correspondence. Essential services such as electricity may be cancelled or disconnected because accounts have been stolen from letter boxes, or unlisted phone numbers may be obtained from a stolen phone account.
- All old or irrelevant mail should be destroyed rather than simply discarded, as occasionally people will go to the lengths of rifling through your rubbish in search of personal information, including credit card details from banking statements.
- Do not answer the door to strangers, even those carrying clipboards. Insist that any caller produces appropriate identification.
- Anyone, particularly those in the public eye, should be wary of disclosing personal information through television or radio appearances or articles pertaining to their personal lives in the print media. Public figures should be cautious about conducting interviews in their home, particularly with accompanying photographs. Disclosing information about one's home in particular gives overzealous fans and potential stalkers the impression of

intimacy with the celebrity and conveys the message that one's private life is not 'off limits'. Valuable clues can be provided in these interviews regarding the precise location of the celebrity's residence.

- Responding to notices in the 'personal' section of magazines and newspapers is always a gamble. While there are likely to be many perfectly legitimate advertisers, these columns are also a means by which the lonely, socially inept individual can have access to a pool of people who are signalling their preparedness for a relationship. Dating agencies present similar problems. Caution is the guiding principle. Guard your personal details, particularly your home and business addresses and phone numbers, resist any pressure for a face-to-face meeting if you feel it is premature and ensure any such meetings are conducted in a public place with the knowledge of a trusted friend.
- Investigate the privacy laws in your jurisdiction by contacting your state's attorney general's office (US and Australia) or in the UK the Lord Chancellor's department or the Home Office. These laws place restrictions on the dissemination of personal information.

Cyberharassment

Be alert to the emerging problem of harassment via the Internet.
- Do not assume any transaction on the Internet is private or confidential.
- Choose online user names with care. Use gender neutral rather than feminine names, and avoid seductive nicknames.
- Play safe and do not flirt online.
- Do not give out personal details about yourself or anyone else, especially your home and workplace addresses and phone numbers.
- Do not respond to flaming (provocation online).
- Remove yourself from any online situation that becomes hostile. Log off.

High risk professions

It is an unfortunate reality that if you work with needy, disordered individuals you are at greater risk of being stalked, as noted in Chapter 6. It is essential that you take steps to protect your privacy and that of your family. In addition to the above measures you should:

- Be cautious about disclosing personal details to patients or clients.
- Ensure you do not leave or display personal information where it can be accessed by patients or clients. Photographs of one's spouse and children that formerly took pride of place in the workstation may now be a liability.
- Avoid divulging home contact details to professional organizations or registries that appear in the public domain.
- Medical practitioners should be aware of confidentiality and privacy issues associated with electronic patient data. For example, with some software programs for prescription writing it is possible to extract clinical information such as the doctor's prescribing and other practice habits, which may be sold to third parties. Given that most computers are attached to a telephone line they can be programmed to dial out overnight and download data to another source without the owner's knowledge. Mudge (2001, p.13) recommends that practitioners seek a statement from their software supplier to this effect:

'(Software supplier) gives an assurance that its product XYZ software contains no facility for covert collection and transfer of either identifiable or de-identified data in any form'.

9

Evading the stalker

Since stalking is not a uniform behaviour with any one consistent motive there can be no single, effective strategy for stopping it. Any approach to the problem of stalking must take account of the individual circumstances, including the nature of any prior relationship between the victim and stalker, the stalker's likely motivation and his mental state, the methods used to harass and the jurisdiction in which the stalking occurs. There are, however, a number of general strategies that have proved useful in combating stalking. The advice in this chapter is necessarily overinclusive. Not all strategies will be appropriate in every case. You will need to assess which of these are relevant to your particular situation. Your friends, family, legal adviser, counsellor or the police can assist with this.

It will hardly seem fair that your stalker has relegated you to a position of having to make significant changes to *your* life, and from time to time victims have responded by refusing to compromise in any way lest it be seen to be 'giving in'. However, this is not a time to be headstrong. Your first priority must be your safety and that of your loved ones. Implementing these strategies is not about giving in but *fighting back*.

Avoid contact and confrontation

Victims can do little if anything to alter directly their stalkers' behaviour, but they can modify their *own* actions. Avoiding all contact with your stalker is a crucial starting point. Once you have conveyed, unequivocally, your wish to be left alone by your stalker *resist the temptation to enter into further dialogue and to appeal to logic*. He has received the message but chooses not to respect your wishes, or he has a major mental illness for which only psychiatric intervention, not negotiation, is likely to effect any change. Each answered phone call, each letter of appeal, even a tirade of abuse on your part acknowledges and rewards your stalker. Your recorded message on your telephone answering machine may reward him. So too can returning the stalker's mail or 'gifts'. To the intimacy seeker, the incompetent suitor and the rejected stalker *any* contact, however negative or tenuous, may offer hope that perseverance will one day be rewarded with a relationship. For the resentful stalker, the gratification is in the knowledge that the communication hit its mark; that the victim has been 'got at'.

Consistently avoiding contact is not an easy plan. You may feel it is 'letting him get away with it', and certainly in the short term it appears that way. However, you must try to tolerate the frustration and the temporary upsurge of activity that may result from bafflement at your stalker's end when his efforts to communicate are thwarted. Otherwise, you may be condemning yourself to a protracted period of harassment. If you are phoned 40 times by your stalker and, out of sheer frustration and anger, you respond to the *next* call with a cavalcade of expletives, then you have effectively just told your stalker that persistence (in this case, *41 phone calls*) will ultimately be rewarded with contact from you, the object of his desire or revenge.

Another reason to avoid contact is that sometimes stalkers will deliberately provoke it to discredit you. If you have a protection order against the stalker (or, as happens, he has succeeded in obtaining one against *you*), contact with your stalker, however provoked, may spell trouble for you. You might even have to defend allegations of breaching the order or find that the police lose interest in investigating your complaints.

You must also refrain from retaliating against your stalker, however justified it may seem. Apart from their potential to be used against you, such attacks place *you* at greater risk. Although homicidal fantasies are understandable and not uncommonly experienced by stalking victims, do not joke about these to others. If physical harm *were* to befall your stalker (and some are predisposed to such outcomes) you might become the prime suspect.

There is really only one way of effecting the 'no contact' approach in the workplace. Either you or the stalker must go, preferably the latter. Antistalking strategies in the workplace will be detailed later. In the case of stalking by a neighbour that persists despite exhausting appropriate legal channels, the most effective strategy, albeit at some considerable cost, is to break all contact by moving to another neighbourhood. This approach should first be discussed with a professional to ensure that your particular circumstances would indeed benefit (see Chapter 13).

Where stalker and victim share children and the stalker has visiting rights, arrange a suitable venue for visitation and exchange. Ask a trusted friend, family member or a professional such as a social worker, if this is more appropriate, to supervise the children on these visits. Do not personally participate.

Finally, if you do meet face to face with your stalker, coincidentally or otherwise, avoid showing any emotion as far as possible. If you are alone, leave the situation, preferably to a busy public place.

Inform others

It is helpful to provide friends and family with information about stalking in order to make your situation and your reaction to it more comprehensible to them. More informed assistance diminishes your risk of feeling alienated and developing major stress related symptoms.

- Try to provide relevant people such as neighbours and work colleagues (or the doorman if you live in secured apartments) with a photograph or a description of the stalker. If they are alerted to the stalker's presence they can take appropriate action such as calling the police or work security staff.
- It is essential that you give explicit instructions to other parties regarding the action to be taken if the stalker makes contact. For instance, ask your neighbours to contact the police or to photograph or video the stalker if he is seen in the vicinity.
- Your work colleagues and neighbours must be instructed not to disclose any personal information about you or your family, a message that may need to be regularly reinforced, particularly with the arrival of new office staff and neighbours.
- Children should never be overlooked in developing action plans, particularly as some are at risk of becoming secondary targets. They should be well grounded in basic safety drills, and the phone numbers of emergency services should be kept beside each phone.
- It is inadvisable for children to collect the mail or any parcels or to answer the phone. Remind them that they must never converse with strangers.

They should not give their name or phone number to any callers, including those who claim to have dialled the wrong number. Instruct them never to divulge your whereabouts or indicate that they are alone at home.

- If appropriate, advise the children's school or day care provider of the situation and security arrangements, and also provide them with a photograph or description of the stalker. Ensure only those individuals authorized by you and who present the requisite identification are allowed to collect your children. It is important to ensure that new teachers are similarly apprized.

- Make sure that someone you trust is informed of your whereabouts and travel plans at all times. Let them know your expected time of return and advise them if this changes. If you live alone arrange for neighbours to look out for your arrival home. Give them a sign (e.g. sound your horn) or call them when you are safely inside.

Documentation

Evidence and documentation are two of your strongest weapons. Document all incidents related to the stalking and retain any evidence, as these will assist the police in their investigations and any future legal proceedings against the offender. It is never too late to start documenting.

- Always keep a pen and paper handy and note the time, date and nature of any incident and the names of witnesses.

- Try to compile a master journal which gives an accurate and reliable chronology of events. It can be difficult for the legal system to appreciate a course of harassing conduct if your records consist of a pile of undated jottings on assorted scraps of paper. This exercise can in itself be distressing for some victims, but ordering events often contributes to a sense of control and mastery and, ultimately, the satisfaction of a successful prosecution.

- In case your diary is lost, stolen or destroyed always make a duplicate copy of this and any other materials or correspondence associated with the stalking, including copies of any police reports filed. Keep these at a separate, secure location such as the home of a reliable friend.

- Ask the police what evidence they require to prosecute your stalker successfully.

- Examples of tangible evidence of harassment include photographic or videotape evidence of the stalker's activities, or both, taped answering machine messages, letters, cards and gifts. Resist the temptation to discard or destroy these immediately, however frightening, embarrassing or repulsive, and certainly *do not return them to their sender*. The latter indicates they were received and, as noted earlier, maintains the 'relationship'.
- Date all answering machine tapes and ensure you have a good stock of replacement cassettes.
- Avoid handling unsolicited material such as letters. Do not staple or tape notes or annotations to them and do not write directly on them. Use Post-it notes as these are less likely to damage the evidence. Insert the material in plastic folders (document sleeves are ideal) and record the date on the outside. Include any envelopes, regardless of whether they are torn. If the police do not wish to retain this evidence, store it in a secure location, such as a lockable cupboard. Inform a trusted friend or relative of your hiding place as stressed victims can forget these things.
- Witness statements are a useful source of objective evidence. Ask any witnesses to stalking incidents if they would be prepared to offer a statement to the police. Note their names, the date and the events witnessed. Ask them to note down what they saw while the incident is still fresh in their memory. Keep a copy with your documents.
- Ensure police are informed of *any* illegal acts that occur during the course of the stalking, such as burglaries or thefts, and retain copies of the police incident report.
- Collect photographic evidence wherever possible, noting dates and circumstances. For instance, photograph any property damage, the stalker's illicit presence in your neighbourhood and any physical injuries sustained by you, your friends or pets. Photograph or note down the licence plate of any suspicious vehicle. *Again, always have pen and paper at hand.*

Security

- Take charge of your environment. If you are in any doubt about the adequacy of your home security have it checked by a professional. In many areas there are special units within the police force that provide confidential home security inspections free of charge. Alternatively, victims of crime support agencies or reputable security companies can assist you. Beware of exploitative security consultants who view this as an opportunity to sell you expensive equipment that may add little to your actual safety. You should obtain three quotes from police licensed security companies – ask to see their security licences and identification.

- Be realistic about your security requirements. Any additions or modifications must suit your needs and finances. It is seldom necessary to spend a large amount of money to achieve an acceptable level of security at home. If you are contemplating a big outlay, especially when your financial means are limited, seek the opinion of the police.
- If you are a tenant, discuss additional security measures with your landlord or the real estate agent managing your property. Landlords are obliged to provide a safe, well-lit residence.

Many of the security measures about the home are simple and inexpensive:

- Trim trees and shrubbery around the house, especially near windows, giving your stalker fewer surveillance points. It will also allow any suspicious activity on your premises to be visible from the street or neighbours' homes.
- Clear rubbish in and around your garage and ensure the garage is adequately lit.
- Install an electric remote control garage door and keep your garage locked at all times.
- Keep your fuse box locked and ensure that there are alternative light sources in your home.
- It is essential that your house number is clearly visible night and day to police or any other emergency services who may be called to your home.
- Draw the blinds at night before switching on the interior lights. Move furniture in front of windows to obscure silhouettes of people inside.
- Do not place phones near windows. If your home is under surveillance phone calls may be used to bring you into the stalker's view.
- Install exterior motion sensor lights at a height that discourages removal and ensure they are adjusted to minimize false alarms triggered by animals.
- Install peepholes in front and back doors.

- Fit timers to the lights so that interior lights will come on at plausible times (e.g. in the kitchen at 6pm and the bedroom at 10pm, adjusting for daylight saving time). You may want to leave the radio on (tuned in to a talkback station), which will also create the illusion of people at home. Furthermore, these techniques can confuse the stalker who may be attempting to establish your routine, and deter potential home invaders.
- Change the locks if your stalker has had access to your keys, and secure your spare keys. Install strong door chains, deadlocks and lockable windows. *However, do not turn your home into a fortress from which there is no escape in the event of a fire or other emergency.* Ensure you have a functioning smoke detector, testing it monthly (this is often overlooked when you are distracted by repeated harassment), and make certain your keys are safe and accessible when you retire at night.
- If at all possible purchase a cellular (mobile) phone to enable you to call for help in an emergency. Choose a low cost phone with cheap line rental and high call costs if the phone is mainly for the purpose of making emergency calls.
- Consider a car phone if your stalker is in the habit of following your vehicle, particularly if you cannot avoid night driving.
- All phones are essentially radio transmitters and can be scanned, so be discreet about the information you disclose in your conversations, employing predevised codes if necessary. This applies also to home phones, including cordless models. Baby monitors can be similarly abused.
- Keep important phone numbers handy; these can be encoded if your phone has an automatic dial feature.
- We are all, to some extent, creatures of habit, but if you are under surveillance or being followed you should try to vary your routine. Take different routes when travelling to and from work. Spend an occasional weekend away with friends, preferably of mixed gender. Such trips also help diminish fear and isolation. The less predictable you become in the watchful eyes of your stalker the better.
- Keep information about your travel plans confidential.
- If you are away for an extended period arrange for deliveries to be suspended and for a friend or neighbour to collect junk mail.

- Try to ensure your car is protected from tampering. Avoid parking in the street and in unsupervised parking lots. If you have no alternative but to leave your car in the open ensure it is in a highly visible public area. Always lock the doors of your vehicle and have a lockable petrol cap. Approach your vehicle with the keys in your hand, and walk around the car before you get in to check the tyres are inflated and there is no obvious damage. Look through the windows and check the interior of the car for tampering or uninvited passengers. Ensure a trusted mechanic regularly services your vehicle.
- When driving, always keep the doors locked and windows up. Be wary of strangers approaching your car and do not give rides to strangers and hitchhikers.
- Do not stop at the scene of a minor traffic accident or breakdown; instead call for help on your cellular phone. Never travel without an inflated spare tyre, adequate tools and a first aid kit. Consider enrolling in a defensive driving course.
- Avoid personalized car licence plates.
- Join your neighbourhood watch programme or form one. These organizations are comprised of neighbours under the supervision of the local police branch. You will be educated about crime in your precinct and strategies to improve neighbourhood safety.
- You must control who has access to your residence. Instruct your family, babysitter or cleaner that nobody is to be admitted to the house without verifying their identity. See that tradesmen or others with legitimate entry to your home are properly supervised.
- Be prepared for a rapid departure. Keep a small bag packed with essentials in a secure place at home, in case you are forced to flee to safety. Include important papers (passport, copies of any protection order and the addresses and phone numbers of key people), credit cards, some ready cash, keys, driver's licence, health care cards, any essential medicines and immediate overnight necessities such as nightwear and toiletries.
- Women's refuges or safe houses and other types of safe temporary accommodation can be accessed by contacting the police, your local victims of crime support agency or crisis phone service. Keep these 24-hour emergency numbers beside your phone.

In the workplace

- Businesses can be held accountable for the safety of employees who are being stalked in the workplace. In consultation with their local police branch, employers should formulate policies and procedures for responding to threats or assaults made by or against their employees. These should be periodically reviewed.
- Make accessible lists of contact persons and crisis and evacuation plans. These should also be available to staff working off site.
- Ensure personnel records at your workplace are securely stored. Reception areas should not be accessible to outsiders when there is no receptionist on duty.
- Before hiring any work applicant references should be checked and enquiries made regarding any history of stalking or aggressive behaviour. Where practicable, contract personnel should be similarly screened.
- Train managers in the appropriate handling of employee terminations and use of resources such as employee assistance programmes, financial planners and counsellors.
- Establish reporting procedures for employees who experience harassing or threatening behaviours in the workplace.
- Require that disordered employees who are engaging in unacceptable behaviour undergo a fitness for duty assessment.
- If appropriate, stipulate that employees and visitors to the work premises wear identification badges.
- Retrieve keys and identification badges from terminated employees.
- If you are being harassed or stalked by a fellow employee, inform your boss or supervisor. If he or she does not respond to your satisfaction, speak to someone more senior. Tell them you will be reporting the offender to the police.
- If you are being stalked by someone from outside your workplace, such as an ex-partner or acquaintance, inform your work superiors and also advise relevant work colleagues. It is essential that your workplace develops safety procedures in the event that your stalker tries to make contact with you there. This is as much for the safety of other workers as for you. Unfortunately, when stalking in the workplace erupts, it is seldom only the primary target that is affected.

- If possible, provide fellow workers, security staff and the doorman with a photograph of the offender. Place it in a prominent position at work and at entry and exit points.
- Provide any other identifying information, such as a description of his car and registration number.
- Ensure nobody gives out any information about you to the stalker or to anyone he may try to impersonate.
- If the stalker is repeatedly calling you at work, ask a co-worker to screen all phone calls. If answering the phone is integral to your work arrange to do other duties until the stalker's activities are halted.
- If possible, arrange access to a more secure car park, with security guard escorts as necessary between your car and workplace.
- If you have a protection order in place ensure that the prohibited zones include your workplace. If not, arrange to have the order varied.
- Regrettably, some stalking victims may suffer discrimination in their workplace as a consequence of the stalking, and some may even lose their jobs because their employers view them as a liability. If you feel you have been treated unjustly at work because you are a stalking victim speak with your union or legal adviser.
- Employers can diminish the potential for 'resentful' stalking within the workplace by encouraging supportive work environments, training employees in solving interpersonal conflicts and ensuring appropriate grievance processes are in place.

Cyberstalking

The cyberstalker, though often an intelligent individual with sophisticated computer skills, is likely to be an emotionally immature and lonely person who seeks attention and intimacy in cyberspace. Typically, the cyberstalker – usually male – 'meets' the victim in a chat room and becomes obsessed with her. He then pursues a close, even smothering relationship with his unwitting target. If rejected, he responds with a campaign of cyberspace harassment, which may extend offline in situations where the victim's contact details have been disclosed.

- Do not even consider divulging personal information to a stranger on the Internet.

- Always regard other users with suspicion. You cannot be certain of 'his' age or gender, and the photograph 'he' sends you may not be 'his' own.
- Be particularly wary of anyone who swears true love after just a few days. Do not meet with this person if you have *any* concerns and certainly only in a public place during daylight hours. Take a friend along, or at least advise family or friends of your plans and the intended meeting place.
- If you are experiencing online harassment, tell the offending party that his communications are unwanted and insist that he stops. Do not respond further and *certainly* do not return the harassment. Leave a hostile situation by logging off or surfing elsewhere.
- Log all evidence at first notice. Download and retain all relevant emails for any subsequent police investigation. Ensure you have saved copies on disk.
- Contact the site administrator of the stalker's Internet service provider or, in the case of email, the system from which the stalker is mailing you. Often sites have an address called postmaster@[ispname].com where problems can be reported.
- If the stalking persists, contact the police. Ask whether you can speak with an officer skilled in investigating computer crimes. Make sure you have concrete evidence (e.g. downloaded messages, chat room transcripts or web page URLs).
- CyberAngels is a network made up of thousands of volunteers, including law enforcement officers, in over 30 countries. The organization monitors the Internet and investigates more than 10 000 harassment complaints a year, as well as offering moral support to victims. This global 'neighbourhood watch' distributes a pamphlet (*Cyberstalking and Internet Online Harassment*) that provides advice on preventing and dealing with cyberstalkers. Their web address, and those of other organizations and resources for victims of cyberstalking, are listed in Appendix 1.

Phone harassment

If your stalker is using the phone to harass you, there are a number of strategies you can employ.
- If you answer a call from your stalker the best thing to do is hang up gently. Slamming the receiver down or screaming can encourage the

stalker. Do not blow a whistle into the phone as the stalker may do the same to you.

- Never answer the phone if it rings immediately after you hang up on your stalker.
- While it may seem logical to change, for a fee, to an unlisted (ex-directory or silent) number, you may be disappointed. More determined and resourceful stalkers can overcome this hurdle, usually by tricking others into disclosing the new number or even reading the number off phone bills if your mail is accessible. In these circumstances, victims understandably view this as a major violation of their privacy, and their confidence in the safety of their environment is further undermined. It may be preferable to connect an answering machine to your phone to intercept and record the stalker's calls. Avoid giving the stalker any vicarious gratification from hearing your voice by asking a friend to record the message on your machine. (This should be a friend of the opposite gender to your stalker, to avoid provoking jealousy.) You should then obtain a *second,* unlisted phone number for all your personal and business calls, being extremely selective about who are made privy to your new listing and insisting that they not disclose this number to anybody under *any* circumstance. It is hoped that the stalker will then continue to call on the original line, oblivious to the fact that a second line exists. His intrusions will be recorded by the answering machine, providing vital objective evidence for any future legal action. Furthermore, because it will no longer be necessary for you to answer that phone line, you will not be rewarding his efforts to contact you. You will be able to answer the phone on the new line with confidence, reducing social and occupational disruptions as well as anxiety reactions triggered by ringing phones.
- Ensure there is a phone connection for your personal line in your bedroom, and further minimize the stalker's intrusions by turning down the volume of the 'stalker line'.
- Keep a cellular phone handy at home in the event of phone line tampering.
- Another useful telecommunications innovation that offers similar benefits is 'caller identification', which displays the number of the caller. This has major limitations, however, in particular the caller's ability to block the

display of his number. Some victims are nevertheless comforted by the additional protection it provides. In the US an 'anonymous call rejection' option can now be added to your phone service, so that if a stalker has a caller identification block he will have to unblock his number (allowing your caller identification to register his call) or your phone will not even ring.

- Other telecommunications innovations may assist stalking victims, such as the ability to retrieve the number of your last caller. In the US, if you receive a hang up call you can dial *69 to establish whether the caller was your stalker. You will be given the last number that called your line and asked if you want to return the call (which you obviously do not). The drawback of this service is that the phone company does not keep records so it cannot be used as legal evidence. Call tracing will overcome this (see below).

- Keep an ample supply of cassettes for the answering machine and replace tapes containing messages with new tapes, to avoid mixing messages or accidentally erasing them.

- You can have your stalker's calls traced through your phone company. This is another important means by which objective evidence of stalking can be collected. Ring your phone company's advice line for nuisance calls, giving the details where known of any suspect. The phone company will advise the police of a successful trace, but they are prohibited from disclosing any identifying information to you. Ensure that you are clear about the length of time your phone trace will be operative. To activate the call tracing service in the US, call the Annoyance Call Bureau of your local phone company to report that you are receiving harassing, obscene or threatening phone calls. To trace the call, dial *57 after each suspicious call. You will be charged between $1 and $2 per traced call, depending on where you live. Once the phone company detects three such calls from the same number, they will send the caller a letter informing him that he is committing an offence and must stop. You can also request that a letter be sent. The phone company will tell you only that they have recorded three matching calls. The actual name and phone number of the caller will be given to the police.

- If you are not satisfied with your phone company's handling of your complaint or request, ask to speak with somebody more senior or the company's security officer. Complaints about your phone service provider may also be directed to the telecommunications ombudsman. In the US complaints may also be directed to the federal communications commission or your state's attorney general's office.

Mail

As has been emphasized earlier, retain all correspondence from your stalker and *do not return it*, unopened or otherwise.

- It is important that *someone* checks the contents of any mail, in case it contains threats or other information that should be acted upon. The best person to do this is not usually the victim, because reading *any* of the stalker's correspondence, let alone that containing threats or other nasty surprises, will create unnecessary distress. It is preferable to redirect the mail to the police or an intermediary such as a work supervisor, the victim being notified only on a 'need to know' basis (e.g. where there is a specific threat to the victim).

Other self-defence strategies

- In addition to the security measures and safety drills outlined earlier training in self-defence techniques may assuage feelings of helplessness and vulnerability. Some stalking victims who have enrolled in self-defence courses (through local councils or gyms) report improved self respect and a sense of empowerment, enabling them to tackle the stalking with renewed determination and assertiveness. Self-defence courses provide instruction in disabling techniques. They do not rely on physical strength or the highly skilled actions of martial arts that take many years to perfect.
- Self defence need not, and should not, entail the carrying of weapons, especially firearms. Innocent people (including children) can be injured by a terrified victim's misuse of weapons, and weapons can be turned against a victim by the stalker. Tragically, weapons may also prove to be a convenient tool for committing suicide for victims too distraught and worn down by their ordeal to see any other options. Victims cannot expect to be treated with leniency if they are responsible for the injury or even death of their stalkers or, worse, innocent persons.

- Weapons such as repellent aerosol sprays (e.g. mace or capsicum) are illegal in many jurisdictions. They are also unreliable in their effects. Some victims have themselves been overcome by the spray's blinding and disorientating effects, rendering them more vulnerable than ever to their stalker, who may remain unaffected.
- Personal handheld duress alarms are legal, however, and victims often feel reassured by them. They must be easily operated and always accessible. Some victims choose to wear them around their necks or on their belts; they are not much use in the average handbag. Police or reputable security firms can advise on these.

Politicians and the media

- If traditional sources of help have failed you, try writing to your local member of parliament, congressman or representative to your state legislature or approach them in person. Consider writing also to the office of the attorney general in your state or territory (or in the UK the Lord Chancellor's department) to alert him or her to the shortcomings of the legal system he or she administers.
- Consider an approach to the media, who are usually keen to publicize the stories of stalking victims, but you must avoid any action that is likely to inflame your stalker. Also, you will in effect be publicly acknowledging him and letting him into your life. You may, however, enhance your chances of a timely and sympathetic response from politicians by informing them that you have approached the media.

Dogs

- These are not always a practical option, but they can be useful as watch-dogs by barking to alert you to a would-be intruder and acting as a deterrent to uninvited visitors. They can be invaluable company, especially if you live alone, and provide greater security when out walking or jogging (though preferably also with another person and during daylight hours).
- Regrettably, some stalkers will target pets. Be alert to food or other foreign items on your premises as they could be baited.

- Ensure that you have a photograph of your dog in case he or she disappears.
- Be warned that training your dog to attack is an intensive undertaking and attacker dogs – like any weapon – have their disadvantages, including the potential to cause harm to innocent individuals.

Bodyguards

Bodyguards, or personal protection specialists, are not a substitute for law enforcement, and the cost of hiring them is prohibitive for most people. If you are contemplating these services make sure you deal with a reputable and suitably qualified company. The police or your victims of crime support organization may be able to recommend somebody suitable.

10

Navigating the criminal justice system in the United States of America

Dr Doreen Orion, MD

Board Certified Forensic Psychiatrist, University of Colorado Health Sciences Center, Denver, Colorado, USA

Police

As a stalking victim, it is up to you to decide if you wish to involve the police. If you do, it is generally best to do so as early as possible in the course of events. *In a life threatening situation, dial 911.* At other times, you can notify your local police precinct if you suspect you are being stalked. If you prefer, you may ask to speak to a female police officer, particularly if the harassment has involved sexual assault. You may also feel more comfortable if a friend, relative or legal adviser accompanies you. Most states have victim/witness assistance services via the district attorney's office, sheriff's department or police department. These victim advocates have been trained to help crime victims negotiate the legal process. They will work with victims regardless of whether charges are filed or a perpetrator is apprehended.

In addition to helping to order your thoughts and place less of a burden on your memory in these stressful circumstances, providing documentation of the stalking will assist the police in their investigations. Remember that stalking often results in a complex trail of behaviours over many months or even years, which can present a formidable task for under-resourced law enforcement agencies. You will need to provide the police with any information you have on the suspect, including a description (with a recent photograph whenever possible), the nature and duration of the harassment, any legal action to date (show them the relevant documents) and any instances of aggression or threats. Be honest with the police about the nature of any prior involvement with the stalker. You should inform the police if you think the stalker has a criminal or psychiatric history and in particular whether you suspect he is in possession of any firearms or other weapons. Insist that a police report is filed, and do not be persuaded otherwise. *Retain a copy of the report* together with your case number, and write down the police officer's name, rank, precinct and badge number for your records. If an arrest is made, you will be sent victim's rights and assistance information, but you can ask for this information at any time.

A police officer generally responds to a call, takes the information and writes a report. Any further investigation is undertaken by a detective. There are very few dedicated units in law enforcement that handle stalking cases and the resources and knowledge within the police force are quite variable. This is partly a consequence of the relatively recent introduction of stalking legislation in the US as a legal avenue for prosecuting perpetrators. Furthermore, most of the crimes police are called to solve are single and circumscribed, not events which are repeated and ongoing. If there are concerns about the manner in which the police are dealing with your complaints you should ask to speak with a more senior officer.

It is helpful if one or two specific detectives can be appointed to your case. Dedicated officers can develop a greater awareness of the stalker's attitude, offending patterns and potential dangers. The victim is spared the frustration of reporting isolated incidents to a different officer on each occasion, who may fail to appreciate their gravity. Stalking is, after all, a *course of conduct,* usually a series of incidents that do not necessarily in themselves constitute criminal behaviour. When reporting the stalker's activities to the police you should, at the very least, begin each report by quoting your case number. Keep this with you at all times.

Reporting the stalking to the police may itself prove effective in ending the stalking. When the identity and whereabouts of the stalker are known, a visit from the police and a stern warning may prove a sufficient deterrent. If the harassment persists, the stalker, in all but a few cases of major mental illness, is clearly demonstrating his *intention* to stalk. His defiance paves the way for more definitive legal intervention. However, a police warning which, in the event of further transgressions, is not followed up with tougher action can give the stalker the message that he is immune to legal sanctions and may even confirm his belief that his behaviour is justified. Always advise the police of any continuing harassment and insist that they take further action along the lines they indicated earlier to the offender.

Ultimately, if you are unhappy with the police response to your situation, a formal complaint can be made to a specific officer in the department designated to deal with public complaints. Smaller departments may not have such a designated officer. Victim advocates can help you lodge a complaint as well. It must be understood, however, that police resources are such that it is unrealistic for crime victims to expect protection around the clock.

Protective injunctions

These are known as restraining orders or protection orders. They do not give your stalker a criminal record. The purpose of these legally binding orders is to convey to the stalker that he is not allowed to continue to harass you. Particular prohibited behaviours are listed on the order: examples include entering or remaining on property that is owned, leased or occupied by you, even when you are not on the premises; visiting your place of work; attending your children's school; and other specified invasions, including the specific distance from you that the stalker is required to remain. Also, if the stalker is harassing you through others or engaging other people to hurt you, this can be proscribed on the order. The precise wording required to protect you will depend on your individual situation. It may help to seek legal advice in this regard, especially where you and your stalker share children to whom he has or is seeking access.

You should at least *consider* obtaining a restraining order against your stalker, as any violation of the order is punishable by law. You must understand, however, that in many circumstances, restraining orders are no more than a paper shield, promoting a false sense of security, since they can be enforced only after the offender has breached them.

Protection orders are most likely to be effective against a reasonable person who has limited emotional investment in his relationship with the victim and no history of violence. Stalkers with erotomanic delusions may well fail to adhere to such an order. Their attachment to the victim is a fantasized one, and orders of this nature are either entirely irrelevant to them or are simply considered a test of their love and devotion.

Protective injunctions may *inflame* ex-partners who have a deep emotional investment in, and overwhelming sense of entitlement to, the victim. The personal humiliation and rage these stalkers experience in response to rejection by their former intimate can be aggravated by the *public* humiliation they perceive when a protection order is imposed. In such cases the order becomes a powerful justification for escalating their stalking activities. *If you do obtain a protective injunction against an ex-intimate, be aware that the period immediately after the issuance of the order is often an emotionally charged time with a heightened risk of physical harm to the victim.* This may also be true in cases where stalker and victim are not ex-intimates.

If you are contemplating a protection order, it is preferable to apply *early* in the course of the harassment. If your stalker has failed to appreciate that his behaviour constitutes a nuisance and a source of distress to you, the order will provide unequivocal evidence of your wishes at the earliest juncture, before his feelings have intensified. The longer the delay in imposing a legal rein on the stalker's behaviour, the less reasonable his reaction to the order is likely to be.

A further disadvantage of these orders is that they are *civil* remedies, not criminal prosecutions. Violations of such orders are usually misdemeanours and when no violence or threat of violence has occurred (or even in some cases when it has) the eventual punishment is unlikely to include a prison sentence. Restraining orders may be permanent or may be issued for finite amounts of time – i.e., they may expire in as little as six months. If you choose to renew the order, you will have to reapply (and undergo the same procedure again) when the order expires.

Furthermore, violations of these orders directly pit the victim against the accused. If possible, it is often preferable to have the stalker charged under stalking statutes (and/or other charges as indicated, such as theft, assault or threats to harm) that may be charged as felonies and usually result in harsher punishments than civil violations. Criminal violations also allow conditions to be placed on the offender, in particular the requirement that he undergoes psychiatric assessment. In many states, once a perpetrator has been convicted of stalking, any future violations of protective orders become felonies. Stalking charges (as opposed to restraining orders) are increasingly being used as a first line approach to stalking as police and the judiciary become more familiar with their application.

To obtain a temporary restraining order you should go to the clerk's office of your county court. Ensure your street address is kept private if it is not already known to your stalker. In preparing your complaint, you (the 'plaintiff') will need to fill in some paperwork that briefly describes the harassment that has occurred and any danger you feel your stalker poses to you. Once the paperwork is completed you will talk to a judge, who, in order to issue an injunction, must be satisfied that you are indeed being harassed or are the object of stalking. Bring any evidence (letters, phone logs, witnesses) you have to make your case to the court. Inform the judge if you believe your stalker (the 'defendant') is in possession of any firearms. The judge will hear the evidence and decide whether there are grounds for the order and what conditions should apply. The judge can then issue a temporary restraining order immediately without your stalker being present. You will then be required to come to court and make your case for a permanent restraining order, usually within a few weeks.

The temporary restraining order will not be enforceable until it is served on the stalker by the police. You can ask the police to notify you when this has taken place. If you do not attend the subsequent hearing to make the order permanent, your complaint will be dismissed and the temporary order will cease to exist. If the stalker has received notice of the order but fails to attend this hearing, you will usually be able to obtain a final order immediately. If you have reason to believe your safety or property is threatened, the court may issue a warrant to have the stalker arrested and brought to court for a hearing. At any point in the proceedings, the stalker may bring an attorney to represent him and can provide evidence and witnesses to dissuade the court from issuing the permanent restraining order.

If the court decides not to make an order or you are unhappy with the terms of the order, you may be able to appeal, depending on the jurisdiction. You can consult an attorney or ask the court. In any case, you should be able to make a new request for a restraining order (if your original request was not granted) if there is a new episode of harassment. You may want to discuss this with a lawyer. The defendant can appeal against the issuance of the order or any of its terms. At any time during the operation of the order, either party can apply to the court to have the order varied, revoked or extended. If you move to another state your order can be enforced there without having to return to court.

It is, of course, essential that if an order of protection is issued it is then enforced. It is a criminal offence (contempt of court) to disobey the conditions of the order, and any breach must be reported to the police. The police should then make an arrest but may only give the stalker a summons to appear in court at a later date. You should insist that the stalker is arrested, but police unfortunately have considerable discretion in these cases.

Protection orders should not be regarded as a routine approach to stalking. There is no universal recommendation about their use, and you are advised to consult with appropriate professionals, such as the police, a lawyer, victims of crime support services or a mental health specialist, to determine whether such an order is likely to be of benefit given the circumstances of your case. Protection orders are generally best viewed as a useful adjunct to other legal proceedings if initiated *early* in the course of stalking. Obtaining an order should not bring with it expectations of protection and resolution of harassment.

Lawyers

The cost of retaining the services of a lawyer may be prohibitive for many stalking victims, but the advantage is that lawyers know the legal system. You may apply for legal advice on a sliding fee scale through legal aid, or there may be programmes through your local law school to provide free services. Neither deals with every legal problem and regrettably many people are ineligible for assistance at reduced cost. These programmes can, however, also provide referral to a local lawyer who may assist you, as can the state Bar Association. If you retain the services of a private attorney, first ask for a written estimate of the cost. If you cannot afford the fees, ask the lawyer to help you pay for assistance through legal aid, which may then fund your lawyer to take the case.

It is often useful to ask your lawyer to send the stalker a letter by certified mail, demanding that he stops stalking immediately or face legal action. This may also be used as an alternative to a restraining order in conveying a very clear message to all but the most disordered of stalkers that the behaviour is unwanted. Some stalkers, most often incompetent suitors, will stop after such a warning.

While most stalking victims are not legally represented in protection order hearings, lawyers can advise on the suitability and terms of these orders. They can also assist you in other legal proceedings pertaining to the stalker's prosecution, advise you on applying for criminal compensation and help with any civil suit should you wish to pursue restitution against the stalker (see below).

Court

The vast majority of victims are novices within the criminal justice system. They often feel overawed at court, and this seemingly unsympathetic and formal environment may reinforce feelings of incompetence and helplessness. You can reduce your anxiety by being informed about how the criminal justice system works and your role in the process.

After you report the stalking to the police, they will investigate the crime. They may recommend that you obtain a restraining order if you have not already done so. The police officer dealing directly with the victim is known as the detective or investigating officer in court proceedings. If you need to communicate further information to the police, contact this officer. The police may not be able to provide anything other than general information regarding the progress of their enquiries if it is considered it may affect the investigation.

If your stalker is charged with an offence (stalking or related offences), he may be interviewed and released on bail, to attend court at a later date. Alternatively, the stalker (or 'defendant') may be held in custody after being charged. He may remain in custody until a court hears the case or he may be released on bail until the case is heard. Contact the investigating officer or prosecutor if you are concerned that the stalker's release will endanger you or your family, and this will be conveyed to the judge at the hearing. There should be a condition on the defendant's bail that he makes no contact with you or your family. Contact the jail at which the stalker is being held and ask that they notify you if the stalker is given bail and is released or escapes.

For the first offence, the stalking charges will be brought in your local county court (unless the defendant was under the age of 18 at the time of the crime, in which case he will usually be tried in a juvenile court). In some jurisdictions, a first stalking offence may be heard in a municipal court. Municipal courts are the lowest in the court hierarchy and are located in many suburbs. Whichever court hears the case, it will be prosecuted by a district attorney or prosecutor, and the stalker will be represented by an attorney or public defender. The judge, who is referred to as 'Your Honour', wears a robe.

Although most first time stalkers are dealt with in the county court system under misdemeanour crime statutes, occasionally these cases will proceed to a higher, district court. This is usually because they are more serious (in legal terms, for example, involving assault with a weapon), or because an appeal has been lodged against the county court judge's ruling. In all of these courts, municipal, county and district, if the case goes to trial, the stalker will be tried before a judge with a jury. A prosecutor from the district attorney's office will prosecute the case. If the stalker is found guilty at trial in the district court, he can appeal to the state court of appeals. This court has no jury, but rather a panel of judges who make their decision strictly on the legal merits of the appeal. Often, a different prosecutor from the state attorney general's office will prosecute this appeal. Neither the victim nor the stalker need appear in court when appeals are heard.

If the defendant pleads guilty, he will do so before a judge. There will be no jury and you may not need to give evidence in court (although you may speak at a sentencing hearing). If he pleads not guilty, your testimony will be required when the case proceeds to trial. This can be particularly problematic in stalking cases, as the victim's presence in court can gratify the stalker's need for contact. The advantage to a stalker's guilty plea is that you will not have to face him in court. The disadvantage is that a defendant pleads guilty only in exchange for a reduced charge or sentence, or both. The prosecutor will discuss this with you before the plea is agreed to, but ultimately it is the prosecutor's decision, not the victim's, whether or not to proceed to trial.

Courts can seem to be unwelcoming places. If possible, take along a supportive friend or family member. A victim/witness advocate can also accompany you. These are professionally trained paid or volunteer support workers. Their services generally include the provision of precourt information, practical and emotional support throughout the legal process and waiting rooms within the court complex. The police or district attorney's office will provide you with their contact details. It is best to arrange this service ahead of the scheduled court hearing so that someone is available for you. A support worker can also show you around when the courts are not in session. If you have special needs, give the prosecutor advance notice. Interpreters can be arranged for victims who do not speak English or those who are hearing impaired.

As noted above, if the case goes to trial and is not plead out, it will be heard before a judge and jury. The defendant will then be found either guilty or not guilty. If the defendant is found not guilty (i.e., he is acquitted), he is immediately set free (if he was in jail) and all charges are dropped. You cannot appeal against this decision. If he is found guilty, the sentence will be determined by the judge and may not be handed down until a later date. Before sentencing the convicted offender, the judge may request a report from a psychiatrist or psychologist. These will generally be professionals who are experienced in the assessment and management of mentally disordered offenders. Their opinion will assist the court in deciding on an appropriate disposition. For stalking, more than many crimes, it is essential that any legal sanctions handed down by the court take into account the nature of any psychiatric condition from which the stalker may be suffering, its amenability to treatment and the best means of delivering that treatment. However essential these psychiatric considerations may be, they should not take priority over you or your family's safety. If you are concerned about the disposition of your stalker, speak with your lawyer, the district attorney prosecuting the case or a victim/witness assistant.

For most first time stalkers presenting before a judge, sentences involve a fine, probation (community correctional order), a deferred sentence or sometimes imprisonment. This is true whether they have been convicted of stalking or any related crimes. Probation will often have conditions attached, such as the requirement that the offender undergoes psychiatric treatment or counselling for drug and alcohol abuse. If the convicted offender does not comply with the conditions of his probation or similar order, he will be returned to court and risk more serious penalties. An offender who breaches a deferred sentence by re-offending may have to serve the remainder of the sentence in prison, but this depends on the severities of the original crime and the subsequent violation. When reporting further stalking activities to the police, remind them that the offender has been convicted of a crime (such as stalking, assault, and so on) and is on probation (or equivalent). Do not assume the police will have this information at their fingertips. You should also contact the stalker's probation officer (whose name and number should be provided to you by the district attorney's office) and inform him or her of any further offences.

If your stalker receives a term of imprisonment and you wish to know his earliest release date, contact the Department of Corrections. You can also be informed of any parole hearing (you can attend and testify if you wish), if parole is to be granted or if the prisoner escapes.

If the accused is acquitted this does not mean the judge or jury disbelieve your story. A number of other factors can influence this decision, particularly the lack of sufficient evidence to prove to the satisfaction of the court or jury that stalking has occurred. It should be noted that the standard of proof for criminal cases is more stringent than that for civil cases. In criminal cases, the onus rests with the prosecution to convince the judge or jury of the defendant's guilt *beyond a reasonable doubt.* In civil cases, such as protection order hearings, the standard of proof is *on the preponderance of evidence.* Even if the stalker is acquitted at trial, the victim may still obtain or retain a civil restraining order.

Criminal injuries compensation

There are a number of different avenues through which victims of crime can receive payments or other financial assistance. The police or district attorney's office will provide you with further information when you report stalking incidents. You can also seek advice and assistance through an attorney. The Victims Compensation Fund can generally cover medical bills and counselling expenses that arise from the crime committed. Often this fund will also cover lost wages, changing locks, fixing broken windows and other property damage resulting from the criminal behaviour of your stalker. There may be a time limit for making claims. Emotional damages (that is, pain and suffering) must be sought through a civil court (see below).

If you are seeking money from the Victims Compensation Fund, you will need to have reported the crime(s) to the police and they will have to agree that the crime has occurred and that your injury or loss resulted from it. It is not necessary for them to have apprehended or charged the perpetrator. You must also be able to show that the crime actually caused your emotional, and in some instances, physical injuries and the fund may seek evidence to support this from your doctor, therapist or an independent specialist. In many areas, the Victims Compensation Fund will require that your therapist is licensed in order for you to recover payment for his or her counselling services.

Some victims do not pursue crimes compensation because they feel unable to face another court appearance. In most jurisdictions, the victim is not required to attend any hearing to receive compensation. For those who must appear in person, however, the victim advocate will be available to assist you during these hearings, and the judges presiding over crimes compensation cases are sensitive to victims and attuned to their needs. You will not have to confront the perpetrator.

It is recognized that the amount awarded can never adequately compensate for the suffering inflicted by a stalker, but for many victims a positive outcome offers validation and a sense of justice, which assists in the rehabilitation process.

You may instead seek restitution by filing a civil suit against the stalker. That is, you can sue your stalker for emotional, physical, financial and punitive damages as a consequence of being stalked. However, you will need to hire an attorney. The local Bar Association can provide the names of personal injury lawyers. Legal advice and representation is costly, but if you retain the services of a lawyer who works on a 'contingency' basis, he or she will recover payment from the sum awarded if the suit is successful. Such civil suits against stalkers are relatively new in the USA and few attorneys have experience with them. Some victims have also successfully turned to such measures to get the stalker to stop his behaviour when criminal sanctions have not been effective.

Victims may also sue for damages in a small claims court, although the amount of money they can recover is limited, usually up to about $5000 depending on the jurisdiction. Victims do not need to be represented by an attorney in a small claims court, although the stalker may bring an attorney. Even if he does not, he will be notified of the hearing. He may not want to miss the chance to meet his victim in a legally sanctioned arena.

11

Navigating the criminal justice system in the United Kingdom

Dr Edward Petch, MBBS, BSc, MSc, MRCPsych, DFP, Dip Crim

Consultant Forensic Psychiatrist, Ealing, Hammersmith & Fulham Mental Health NHS Trust, Uxbridge Road, Southall, Middlesex, UK

The Protection from Harassment Act 1997 (referred to throughout this chapter as the Act) was introduced 'in order to protect persons from harassment and similar conduct'. This chapter describes the new Act and explains how it might be used by stalking victims. The chapter also sets out the process entailed for victims who are considering involving the police and the courts and what might happen at each stage. This is summarized in the flow diagram in Appendix 4.

There is purposefully no legal definition of stalking or harassment in the UK Act. It was thought that if harassment had been defined, then some stalkers might adapt their behaviour to ensure that it remains within the law. To avoid this trap, the Act aims to prohibit all behaviour that has a particular effect on you, and it is the *effect that the harassment has on you* which has been defined. In this way, the pitfalls and loopholes observed with many of the earlier laws in other jurisdictions throughout the world have been avoided.

The extent of stalking in the UK

When the Act was introduced, although there was considerable public concern regarding stalking, there were no population based studies from the UK exploring the extent of stalking. However, there were indications from the United States and Australia that it might be a widespread problem. Since then the 1998 British Crime Survey has been completed (see Chapter 2), and the results indicate that stalking in the UK is just as widespread as it is in these other countries.

UK antistalking legislation: Protection from Harassment Act 1997

In the UK, as in other parts of the world, it took several high profile cases and the subsequent public outrage and media pressure to mobilize the government. Several prominent lobby groups (for example, the National Anti-stalking and Harassment Campaign and the Suzy Lamplugh Trust) campaigned vigorously for effective prohibition of stalking. After consultation the Home Office became convinced of the need for new legislation and drafted a new act.

The Protection from Harassment Act 1997 for England, Wales and Northern Ireland came into force in June 1997. It is often referred to in the British media as the antistalking law, although it was designed to protect from a far wider range of behaviour, such as nuisance neighbours and racial abusers. It does not define harassment, and it is up to jurors and magistrates as reasonable people to decide whether any given behaviour amounts to harassment or stalking. The Act created two criminal offences: a low level offence in section 2 (criminal harassment) and a higher level offence in section 4 (putting people in fear of violence). The Act is set out in full in Appendix 2.

Prohibition of harassment

Harassment is prohibited in section 1:

A person must not pursue a course of conduct:
(a) which amounts to harassment of another, and
(b) which he or she knows or ought to know amounts to harassment of the other.

Harassment is further defined in section 7(2): *references to harassing a person include alarming the person or causing the person distress.* (Harassment, alarm and distress caused by threatening, abusive or insulting behaviour are words used in the Public Order Act 1986. The words threatening, abusive and insulting do not appear in the Protection from Harassment Act 1997, mainly because stalkers may not intend to be threatening, abusive or insulting but may nevertheless be causing harassment, alarm or distress.) *A course of conduct must involve conduct on at least two occasions* (section 7(3)). The two or more incidents do not have to be similar but must contribute to the overall course of conduct. The more incidents complained of, presumably the less harassing they would need to be to secure a conviction: e.g. loitering outside on two occasions may not be sufficient to secure conviction, but if it occurred repeatedly day after day it might.

Section 1(2) states:

> . . . the person whose course of conduct is in question ought to know that it amounts to harassment of another if a reasonable person in possession of the same information would think the course of conduct amounted to harassment of the other.

Any behaviour that a defendant knows, or ought to know, amounts to harassment is prohibited. The issue of intent is therefore determined not by the defendant (the stalker) but by the reasonable person (perhaps a magistrate or juror). If you believe you have been harassed, and a reasonable person agrees, further definition is unnecessary: for the purposes of a court, harassment is proved and the intent of the defendant is irrelevant.

Offence of harassment

Section 2 states:

> A person who pursues a course of conduct in breach of section 1 is guilty of an offence.

The three elements of section 1 (course of conduct, harassment, ought to know) would have to be proved beyond reasonable doubt to secure a conviction. Harassment under section 2 is a summary offence (triable in a magistrates court), with a penalty of up to six months' imprisonment, a maximum fine of £5000, or both.

Sections 1 and 2 are so worded that they may be used to cover different situations, e.g. public disorder or racial or sexual harassment.

Offence of putting people in fear of violence

Section 4 sets out the higher level offence:

(1) A person whose course of conduct causes another to fear, on at least two occasions, that violence will be used against him is guilty of an offence if he knows or ought to know that his course of conduct will cause the other so to fear on each of those occasions.

(2) For the purposes of this section, a person whose course of conduct is in question ought to know that it will cause another to fear that violence will be used against him on any occasion if a reasonable person in possession of the same information would think the course of conduct would cause the other so to fear on that occasion.

Section 4 is an indictable offence (that is, triable in a magistrates or crown court – see later). Conviction in the crown court may result in up to five years' imprisonment, an unlimited fine, or both. This offence of putting people in fear of violence requires the victim to experience actual fear *of violence* and therefore limits this section to more serious conduct irrespective of any other distress experienced by the victim.

The Act makes both higher and lower level offences immediately arrestable without the need for a warrant, which enables the police to remove the stalker promptly to a place of custody and away from the victim. The Act also gives the police the power to search the suspect's property for any evidence of obsession with the victim (such as photographs or letters).

Restraining orders and injunctions

In both criminal and civil courts the behaviour of your stalker can be restrained by an order: in the criminal court under section 5 of the Act this is called a restraining order, and in the civil court under section 3 it is called a restraining injunction. Orders and injunctions essentially serve the same purpose: to legally prohibit your stalker from certain behaviours.

The restraining order (under section 5) can be issued by a criminal court immediately after the conviction of a person on either of the two criminal offences described above. The order may impose limits on the future behaviour of your stalker and may spare you from taking separate civil proceedings to obtain an injunction. A restraining order may therefore remove the potential trauma and expense of a second court appearance. There are, however, occasions when you might need to resort to the civil courts, as will be discussed later.

The injunction and restraining order can be tailored to your specific circumstances at the discretion of the court. For example, the court could ban your stalker from sending flowers, standing within a certain distance of your house or telephoning for a certain period. A 'typical' restraining order is reproduced in Appendix 3. Breach of a restraining order is both a contempt of court and a criminal offence; the police have powers of arrest and can return the offender to court. The penalty for such a breach is up to five years' imprisonment, an unlimited fine, or both. This may provide a real incentive for the stalker to stop, but if he does not desist the courts can promptly be informed that the behaviour is continuing.

In some cases restraining orders and injunctions seem to have little impact on the stalker. Indeed, a restraining order might occasionally serve to strengthen the resolve of the stalker (e.g. in those with a psychiatric disorder such as erotomania). This may briefly increase the risk to you. Restraining orders are probably most effective and most useful when they are issued early in the course of harassment and when the stalker does not have any major mental disorder nor history of violence.

To provide the greatest possible protection, the conditions on restraining orders and injunctions need to be tailored to the specific circumstances. This means that the courts must know as much about the case as possible. Generally, victim evidence is becoming more important to those deciding the sentence. This is particularly important when the court considers whether or not to grant a restraining order and, if so, the duration of the order and the conditions that should be imposed. The length of the order may not be specified, in which case the order may be in force until a further order is made by the court (essentially, until further notice). You can feed information into the process and carefully consider the conditions you would wish to see in the order. It is vital that you are informed of the conditions after any order is made. If you are not informed, speak with the investigating officer. Such information will enable you to report back to the police if any breaches occur.

Breach of the conditions of a restraining order or restraining injunction is an arrestable criminal offence and carries a maximum penalty of five years' imprisonment or an unlimited fine, or both, in a crown court (or up to six months' imprisonment and £5000 fine, or both, in a magistrates' court). The major difficulty with restraining orders is that they are not always effectively policed. Offenders who ignore these orders may not always be returned to court, but they should be. When they are, the penalties imposed have been customarily minor (e.g. a small fine). As the courts become more familiar with the Act and these orders, it is hoped that they will become more effective in protecting victims from harassment.

Scotland

The Protection from Harassment Act 1997 does not extend to Scotland in the same way. There is a separate provision for Scotland, whereby a victim may make a claim to a civil court (an action of harassment under section 8) if it can be shown they have been harassed. The court can grant damages and a nonharassment order if further protection is required, breach of which can attract a penalty of up to five years' imprisonment. A nonharassment order has to be obtained and then breached before criminal penalties apply.

Strengths of the Protection from Harassment Act 1997

The strength of the Protection from Harassment Act 1997 is that it is a widely drafted law, so that it covers a broad range of behaviours. It also manages to exclude nonharassing legitimate behaviour and offers remedies to victims in both civil and criminal courts. Previous laws which have failed to offer such a range of remedies for different situations have floundered and have not been effective in curbing this very varied form of antisocial behaviour. The Act, on paper at least, appears to be one of the strongest in the world.

In neither the higher nor the lower level offence is the word harassment or 'stalking' defined, although to constitute a course of conduct there must be conduct on at least two occasions (section 7). As earlier noted, the approach whereby prohibited behaviour is listed (which might allow a stalker to extend his behaviour outside the list) was avoided. The courts are therefore obliged to view the harassment from the *victim's* perspective. The behaviour amounts to harassment if you perceive it as such and any reasonable person would agree. This victim-centred approach also removes the opportunity for a stalker to argue that what amounts to harassment for one person may not be perceived as such by somebody who is perhaps more resilient.

The criminal justice system and the Protection from Harassment Act 1997

The vast majority of victims are novices within the criminal justice system. They may feel overawed in court, and this seemingly unsympathetic and formal environment may reinforce feelings of incompetence and helplessness. You can reduce your anxiety by being informed about how the criminal justice system works and your role in the process. This section describes the criminal justice system in the UK and what you as a victim might expect at the various stages of proceedings against your stalker.

Victims

Having made a complaint about harassment, you may decide to withdraw. You may have been threatened by the offender, subjected to pressure from friends and family or even reconciled with the offender. Alternatively, you may have decided to pursue the matter through the civil courts or feel just too frightened to go ahead with a trial and all it entails. The Crown Prosecution Service (CPS) can sometimes proceed and introduce your evidence without requiring your further co-operation. You may not have to give evidence, and you do not necessarily need to prove that you are afraid in order to avoid giving evidence. If you do decide to withdraw you will need to make a statement to that effect, which the police will help you prepare. That will need to include:

- your reasons for withdrawing;
- details of the original allegations;
- whether the original offence occurred or not;
- whether you just want proceedings to stop;
- whether you are under any pressure to withdraw and if so from whom;
- who you have discussed the case with;
- whether you have started civil proceedings;
- what impact the withdrawal will have on you life.

This information will allow the CPS to consider what action to take in the light of your withdrawal. It is very unlikely that you will be compelled to give evidence against your wishes. If the CPS decides to discontinue your case (even if you have not withdrawn the complaint), the CPS and the police should consult with you first.

If you have been intimidated by the offender to withdraw your complaint, you should inform the police. The police will then consider making an arrest under section 51 of the Criminal Justice and Public Order Act 1994. This prohibits intimidation of a witness.

In the criminal courts cases are brought against offenders not by you but by the prosecution acting on behalf of Her Majesty (or Regina, essentially the state); hence the case is known as *R v S*, where 'S' is the name of your stalker. This means that you are not forced to assume responsibility for prosecuting, and it is not *you* pitted against the stalker but the state.

Lawyers

In the UK there are two types of lawyers: solicitors (who represent and act for their clients) and barristers. Barristers are instructed by solicitors to present the case for the defence in court or are instructed by the CPS to present the case for the prosecution. They are sometimes called 'counsel'.

Victims of crime do not necessarily have the right to legal representation. Lawyers can be expensive, but a lawyer who knows this area of law may offer a significant advantage. Free legal assistance is now very limited, because it is means tested. Advice can be obtained from various quarters, including the Citizen's Advice Bureau, who can provide names of reliable local lawyers. The Law Society may also assist in recommending suitable lawyers (see Appendix 1 for contact details).

Police response

In an emergency, *dial 999*. If you think you are being stalked, involve the police at the earliest opportunity. You can talk to a female officer if you prefer, and it is often helpful to take along a trusted friend or relative for support. Produce all the evidence you have collected – documents, previous court orders, diary of incidents, photographs, tapes and 'gifts' to support your claim. Wherever possible, try to keep your own copies of any evidence you provide to the police. The police will also need information about the stalker where available – a description, photograph, address, any known criminal or psychiatric history and any knowledge of his involvement with weapons. The police will need to know your relationship, if any, to the person stalking you. Do not despair if your information is limited, because the police will investigate in any event. However, the more evidence you can produce, the easier it will be for the police to intervene. The police should also be able to assist you in collecting further evidence if this is required.

Some police officers are not yet familiar with the finer points of the anti-stalking laws, and if you do not feel confident that your case is being handled appropriately, you can ask to speak to a more senior officer. If you are still concerned about the way your case is being handled there are avenues for complaint (see Appendix 1).

It is important that your allegations are formally reported as a crime. Keep a copy of the report, the report number, the officer's name, rank, number and station and also a record of when and where you made the report. You should be given information for victims explaining your rights.

It is helpful if one or two specific officers can be appointed to your case. Dedicated officers can develop a greater awareness of the stalker's attitude and offending patterns and the potential dangers. The victim is spared the frustration of having to report isolated incidents to a different officer on each occasion. Police who are unfamiliar with your circumstances may fail to appreciate the seriousness of these incidents. Stalking is, after all, a *course of conduct*, usually a series of incidents that may not necessarily of themselves constitute criminal behaviour. Every time you file a report, give your case number (it helps to keep this close at hand). When you call the police, the call will be assigned a unique reference number. Although the police may not be willing to give this number to you, ask how you can at some future point refer the police to this call. Enter the time and a summary of each call in your log book.

The police are sometimes unsure of their powers of enforcement and may be ambivalent about using them. The effectiveness of the police response may be enhanced by a recent initiative, the publication of guidance for police officers dealing with stalking cases (Brown, 2000). This information is essential for investigating officers as there are many pitfalls on the road towards successful prosecution. (You can access this document via the website address so you know what the police are supposed to do.) For example, in order to prove a course of conduct, clear police records of each incident need to be kept, together with records of any police warnings issued. If the behaviour does persist after a warning, it must be followed up by further action, so it is important that you tell the police if harassment is continuing. Warnings also ensure that if a suspect continues to stalk, the warning can later be used as evidence in court that he knew that his behaviour amounted to harassment.

It is a responsibility of the police to provide a report on your case to the CPS, which decides whether the offender should be prosecuted. The police need as much information as possible to reach this decision. These data may also be needed to oppose bail. The information may include:

- the facts of the case;
- previous convictions;
- the history of the relationship between stalker and victim;

- use of a weapon;
- the use of threats, intimidation or violence;
- any evidence of planning in the harassment;
- details of previous warnings given and police contact;
- the involvement of any third party;
- current status of your relationship with your stalker;
- your view on prosecution.

Whether or not the case is pursued, the police should provide you with details of other agencies that can provide you with help, support and advice. This might include local authority agencies such as social services and housing, the Citizen's Advice Bureau, local women's refuges, rape crisis centres and victim support services (see websites and contact details, Appendix 1).

Charging and prosecuting

It is very frustrating when the police do not bring what you consider to be the correct charge. There can be many reasons for this, including a lack of effective communication between the police and the CPS. In the 1998 British Crime Survey, in some cases that were clearly offences against section 4, offenders were only prosecuted under section 2, as it was thought to be easier. This was not actually true, as proceedings against section 2 and section 4 appeared to be equally likely to result in a conviction (Harris, 2000). In most cases, however, decisions regarding charges were made according to the seriousness of the complaint. Some officers may not be aware of the differences between sections 2 and 4, and may be poorly informed about how to use the Act. The CPS has maintained that charging under both sections 2 and 4 would ensure that when the more serious charge is not proved, it would be possible to fall back on the lesser charge. This is not strictly necessary because section 4(5) of the Act states that if someone charged under Section 4 is found not guilty, they can be found guilty under section 2.

In those cases that are dropped or where police do not bring charges, the police may advise you that there is an option to pursue a claim in the civil courts. In some cases this may bring advantages e.g. a lower standard of proof is required and damages may be awarded. An injunction could still be imposed.

Bail

When your stalker is charged he may be interviewed and released back into the community on bail, to attend court at a later date. Alternatively, after being charged the stalker (by now the 'defendant' or 'accused') may be held on remand in custody. He may remain in custody until a court hears the case or he may be later released on bail until the case is heard. Contact the investigating officer if you are concerned that the stalker's release will endanger you or your family, and the police will advise the magistrate accordingly. There should be a condition on the defendant's bail that he makes no contact with you or your family.

The effectiveness of the Act would be greatly enhanced if police and the courts were very careful when considering bail applications, as release in some cases may lead to a resumption or escalation of the harassment. If defendants are given bail it is important that the court considers imposing conditions on that bail. Conditions can ensure the offender's attendance at court and can keep him away from you. You should be informed of any bail conditions, and the police should also take whatever steps possible to ensure that there is no further harassment. These might include providing additional security measures, regular visits from police and helping you contact alternative accommodation or refuges where necessary. Bail can be opposed.

Criminal courts

In the first instance, the stalking allegations will be heard in a magistrates' court (unless the defendant was under 18 years at the time of the offences, in which case he will usually be tried in a youth court). Magistrates' courts are the lowest in the court hierarchy and are located in many suburbs and regional centres. Neither the prosecuting nor defending lawyers nor the presiding magistrate (who is referred to as 'Your Worship') wear wigs or gowns.

Although most first time stalkers are currently dealt with in the magistrates' court, occasionally cases where the defendant is charged with the higher level offence under section 4 of the Act (putting the victim in fear of violence) will proceed to a higher court. This is usually because in legal terms they are more serious (e.g. involving assault with a weapon) or because an appeal has been lodged against the magistrate's decision. In these courts (the crown court) the stalker will be tried before a judge (referred to as 'Your Honour'), with or without a jury. The case will be prosecuted by a lawyer (usually a barrister acting on the instructions of the CPS). The defendant will also have a legal team. Judges and lawyers in the crown court usually wear wigs and gowns.

If the defendant pleads guilty you may not need to give evidence in court, but if he pleads not guilty your testimony may be required. This can be particularly problematic in stalking cases as the victim's presence in court can gratify the stalker's need for contact. If the prospect of face-to-face contact with your stalker (and perhaps his family) in the courtroom distresses you, tell the police, the witness service, the CPS or your lawyer. Applications can be made to the court for consideration of alternative arrangements under the Youth Justice and Criminal Evidence Act 1999. These arrangements include giving evidence from a place other than the courtroom by closed-circuit television, the use of screens to remove the defendant from your direct line of vision or clearing the court beforehand.

Courts can be rather unwelcoming and imposing places. If possible, take along a supportive friend or family member. Often courts provide professionally trained volunteer support workers or a witness service for those who are unfamiliar with court procedures. This service generally includes the provision of precourt information, practical and emotional support throughout the court hearing and waiting rooms within the court complex. The police or court information desk will provide you with contact details. It is best if you can arrange this service ahead of the scheduled court hearing so that someone is available for you. A support worker can also show you around when the courts are not in session to familiarize you with the layout of the court.

If you have special needs, give the police or prosecutor advance notice. Interpreters can be arranged for victims who do not speak English or those who are hearing impaired.

If the defendant pleads guilty, the court can proceed direct to the sentencing stage. If the defendant pleads not guilty, he will be tried either in the magistrates' court or in the crown court before a jury if the charges are more serious. If found not guilty (acquitted) the defendant is usually free to leave court. If the defendant is found guilty (convicted), the magistrate or judge may request before sentencing a report from the probation service or from a psychiatrist or psychologist. These are generally professionals experienced in the assessment and management of mentally disordered offenders. Their opinion will assist the court in deciding on appropriate action. For stalking in particular it is essential that any legal sanctions handed down by the court take account of the nature of any psychiatric condition the stalker may be suffering, its amenability to treatment and the best means of delivering that treatment. However essential these psychiatric considerations may be, they should not take priority over you or your family's safety. If you are concerned about the way in which the court deals with your stalker, speak with your lawyer, the CPS lawyer or the police.

For most of first time stalkers presenting before a magistrate, sentences involve a fine, a probation order, a community service order, a suspended prison sentence or a conditional discharge. Probation will often have conditions attached, such as the requirement that the offender undergoes psychiatric treatment. A restraining order can also be added (see below). If the convicted stalker does not comply with the conditions of his probation or similar order he will be returned to court and risk more serious penalties. An offender who breaches a suspended sentence by reoffending is likely to serve the remainder of the sentence in prison. You should therefore report further stalking activities to the police, but you need to remind them that the offender has been convicted of stalking and is on probation (or equivalent). Do not assume the police will have this information at their fingertips.

If your stalker receives a term of imprisonment and you wish to know his earliest release date, write to the local probation office. If you specifically want to know whether he is to be granted parole, contact the parole board.

If the accused is acquitted, it does not mean the magistrate, judge or jury disbelieves your story. A number of other factors can influence this decision, particularly the lack of sufficient evidence to prove to the satisfaction of the court or jury that stalking has occurred. It should be noted that the standard of proof for criminal cases is more stringent than that for civil cases. In criminal cases, the onus rests with the prosecution to convince the magistrate, judge or jury of the defendant's guilt *beyond reasonable doubt,* while in the civil courts guilt is determined *on the balance of probabilities.*

Civil courts

Those who are or who may be victims of harassment can make a claim to the civil courts (i.e. the local county court or the high court), for an injunction or damages, or both. The Protection from Harassment Act 1997 therefore provides both a criminal and a civil remedy. There is sometimes a degree of uncertainty about when it might be appropriate to use the criminal measures and when it might be more appropriate to use the civil remedies. There is no hard and fast rule, and you are advised to seek appropriate legal advice. Unless you particularly want to go down the civil route, in most cases criminal proceedings are likely to be more appropriate.

There are, however, advantages in using the civil courts. The civil court has the power to award you damages, and, because the standard of proof is lower in civil compared with criminal courts, stalking is easier to prove. Civil courts can also impose restraining injunctions (under section 3 of the Act) to prohibit your stalker from continuing to harass you.

Essentially, the definition of harassment is the same for both civil and criminal proceedings, and this is set out in section 1 of the Act; they are dealing with the same degree of gravity. In both criminal and civil courts the defendant can be restrained by an order: as noted earlier, in the civil court under section 3 it is called a restraining injunction, and in the criminal court under section 5 it is called a restraining order. However, a major difference is that in section 3 an application can be made to a civil court for a restraining injunction *before* a course of conduct has developed. It can therefore be instituted before criminal proceedings would be possible.

The civil court does not give out punishment to the defendant; this may be an attractive option if you don't wish to brand your stalker a criminal. This is sometimes the case in situations involving ex-partners or friends. Historically, the civil courts have been the usual forum for the settling of private, rather than criminal, disputes. Civil courts can award damages for financial loss, trauma or anxiety.

Proceedings and rules of evidence

In some cases it might be possible for stalkers to use proceedings themselves in the furtherance of their stalking activities. By defending themselves in court against any charges, they can exercise their right to cross examine *you*. To be exposed to your stalker in this way is harassing in itself. There are occasions when victims of crime can be protected from such exposure, under the Youth Justice and Criminal Evidence Act 1999, but it is not clear whether these provisions have yet been used in harassment trials. As noted above, protections include the use of screens, video cameras, television links outside court, cross examination conducted on screen and clearing the public gallery. Alternatively, sections 23, 25 and 26 of the Criminal Justice Act 1988 do give courts the discretion to admit written statements as evidence instead of oral evidence if you are in fear. You can ask a lawyer or the police to explore this possibility. In due course it might be possible to prevent certain types of defendants from personally examining their victims.

Courts are obliged to comply with the Evidence Act 1898, which means they are allowed to hear evidence relating only to current charges and may not take into consideration previous convictions or the fact that the behaviour has occurred in the context of long-standing harassment. If a defendant has previous convictions for harassment, that in itself would be evidence that he knows that his behaviour amounts to harassment. Although it would seem logical for that evidence to be put before the court, under current arrangements it is not possible. In these cases relatively small penalties may be imposed for the current offences, and the course of conduct may go unacknowledged. Given that, by its very nature, stalking may be a long-term pattern of behaviour, the accumulation of which causes damage to victims, it should perhaps be possible for factual evidence related to the charges currently before the court to be allowed or for the law regarding evidence to be changed in this respect. It is important that at the very least your evidence about previous harassment is put before the court at the *sentencing* stage (that is, *after* the defendant has been convicted).

Psychiatric assessment of the stalker

Few antistalking laws contain specific provisions for psychiatric assessment of offenders, despite the recognition that mandatory assessment and treatment may prevent further offending in cases where the stalking is driven by underlying psychiatric disorder. There is no compulsory psychiatric assessment and treatment for stalkers after their conviction. The Act does not just cover stalking behaviour but various forms of harassment, and it is considered inappropriate for psychiatric assessment to be ordered in every case. The matter has been left to the discretion of the courts, which already have adequate powers to order psychiatric assessments and treatment where necessary. If a victim suspects the presence of a mental disorder in her stalker, the court should be made aware of this.

Sentences

The 1998 evaluation of the effectiveness of the Act found that the most frequent disposition following conviction was a conditional discharge (40% of cases). A quarter of those convicted received community sentences and a relatively small number (13%) were imprisoned. Prison does not always solve the problem, especially if the stalker is mentally disordered and incarceration fails to address this. Also, a small number of offenders will continue to harass their victim by writing letters or making threatening phone calls from prison. If this happens to you, contact the police and inform them that the harassment is continuing. You can also write to the governor of the prison (the address of the relevant prison establishment and governor can be obtained from the Prison Service website) or contact the Prison Service victim's helpline (see Appendix 1 for details). Ensure the prison is informed of any current restraining order.

Compensation

Compensation to victims of crime is available either through the civil courts or through the criminal injuries compensation authority. The process tends to be lengthy and arduous. You will need to prove fault or blame and that you have suffered as a consequence (whether physical or psychological/psychiatric injury). This issue is decided by a judge in a civil court on the balance of probabilities. To receive compensation from the criminal injuries compensation authority you will need to make an application. This information is posted on their website (Appendix 1), or ask the police for details. You will need to show that you have suffered and that your suffering occurred as a consequence of being stalked. This may not be straightforward in every case. It is unlikely that any amount of money could ever fully compensate for what you have had to endure, but the process of being awarded compensation, however small, might offer some validation and sense of justice.

12

Navigating the criminal justice system in Australia

Police

Police should be involved as early as possible in the course of events. *In a life threatening situation dial 000.* At other times, if you suspect you are being stalked you should promptly notify your local police branch. You can ask to speak to a female police officer, particularly if the harassment has involved sexual assault. You may feel more comfortable if a friend, relative or legal adviser accompanies you. In addition to helping to order your thoughts and place less of a burden on your memory in these stressful circumstances, providing documentation will assist the police in their investigations. Remember that stalking often results in a complex trail of behaviours over many months or even years, which can present a formidable task for under-resourced law enforcement agencies. You will need to provide the police with any information you have on the suspect, including a description (with a recent photograph wherever possible), the nature and duration of the harassment, any legal action to date (show them the relevant documents) and any instances of aggression or threats. Be honest with the police about the nature of any prior involvement with the stalker. You should inform the police if you think the stalker has a criminal or psychiatric history and, in particular, whether you suspect he is in possession of any firearms or other weapons.

Insist that an incident report is filed, and do not be persuaded otherwise. *Retain a copy of the report* together with your file number, and write down the police officer's name, rank, station and number for your records. Make sure you are given a copy of victim's rights and assistance information, which accompanies the incident report in many jurisdictions.

There are currently no dedicated units within the Australian police force that handle stalking cases, and the resources and knowledge within the police force are quite variable. This is partly a consequence of the relatively recent introduction in this country of stalking legislation as a legal avenue for prosecuting perpetrators. Furthermore, most of the crimes police are called to solve are single and circumscribed, not events which are repeated and ongoing. If there are concerns about the manner in which the police are dealing with your complaints you should ask to speak with a more senior officer. You may prefer to contact the police victim advisory service in your state or territory (the local police will provide these details).

It is helpful if one or two specific officers can be appointed to your case. Dedicated officers can develop a greater awareness of the stalker's attitude and offending patterns and the potential dangers. The victim is spared the frustration of having to report isolated incidents to a different officer on each occasion. Police who are unfamiliar with your circumstances may fail to appreciate their seriousness. Stalking is, after all, a *course of conduct*, usually a series of incidents that do not necessarily of themselves constitute criminal behaviour. When reporting the stalker's activities to the police you should, at the very least, preface each report by quoting your file number. Keep this beside your phone.

Reporting the stalking to the police may in itself be effective in ending the stalking. When the identity and whereabouts of the stalker are known, a visit from the police and a stern caution may prove a sufficient deterrent. If the harassment persists, the stalker, in all but a few cases with major mental illness, is clearly demonstrating his *intention* to stalk. His defiance paves the way for more definitive legal intervention. However, a police warning which, in the event of further transgressions, is not followed up with tougher action can give the stalker the message that he is immune to legal sanctions, and it may even confirm the stalker's belief that his behaviour is justified. Always advise the police of any continuing harassment and insist that they take further action, along the lines they spelled out earlier to the offender.

Ultimately, if you are unhappy with the police response to your situation a formal complaint can be made to the police ombudsman's office. Victims of crime support services can assist you in lodging this. It must be understood, however, that police resources are such that it is unrealistic for crime victims to expect protection around the clock.

Protective injunctions

These are also known as restraining orders, restraint orders, intervention orders, apprehended violence orders or non-molestation orders. They do not give your stalker a criminal record. The purpose of these legally binding protection orders is to inform the stalker that he is not allowed to continue to harass you. Particular prohibited behaviours are listed on the order, such as entering or remaining on property that is owned, leased or occupied by you, even when you are not on the premises, or attending your children's school and other specified invasions. Also, if the stalker is harassing you through others or engaging other people to hurt you, this can be proscribed on the order. The precise wording required to protect you will depend on your individual situation. It may help to seek legal advice in this regard, especially when you and your stalker share children to whom he has or is seeking access.

You should at least *consider* obtaining a protection order against your stalker, as any violation of the order is punishable by law. You must understand, however, that in some circumstances they can be no more than a paper shield, promoting a false sense of security, since they can be enforced only once the offender has breached them. Protection orders are most likely to be effective against a reasonable person who has limited emotional investment in his relationship with the victim and no history of violence. Stalkers with erotomanic delusions may well fail to adhere to such an order. Their attachment to the victim is a fantasized one, and orders of this nature are either entirely irrelevant to them or are simply considered tests of their love and devotion.

Protective injunctions may *inflame* ex-partners who have a deep emotional investment in, and overwhelming sense of entitlement to, the victim. The personal humiliation and rage these stalkers experience in response to rejection by their former intimate can be aggravated by the *public* humiliation they perceive when a protection order is imposed. In such cases the order becomes a powerful justification for escalating their stalking activities. *If you do obtain a protective injunction against an ex-intimate be aware that the period immediately after the issuance of the order is often an emotionally charged time with a heightened risk of physical harm to the victim.*

If you are contemplating a protection order it is preferable to apply *early* in the course of the harassment. If your stalker has failed to appreciate that his behaviour constitutes a nuisance and a source of distress to you the order will provide unequivocal evidence of your wishes at the earliest juncture, before his feelings have intensified. The longer the delay in imposing a legal rein on the stalker's behaviour the less reasonable his reaction to the order is likely to be.

A further disadvantage of these orders is that they are a *civil* remedy, not a criminal prosecution. They rarely result in prison sentences and in most jurisdictions pit the victim against the accused. It is often more appropriate to have the stalker charged under stalking statutes (and/or other charges as indicated, such as theft, assault or threats to kill). This approach diffuses some of the volatility encountered in civil interventions initiated by victims because the criminal charges are brought about by the police. It may also reduce the demands on the victim in the legal process, including face-to-face contact with the stalker.

As police and the judiciary become increasingly familiar with their application, stalking charges (as opposed to protective injunctions) are becoming more useful as a first line approach to stalking. Most importantly, prosecution under stalking laws offers greater flexibility in sentencing and more serious penalties than civil approaches. These penalties allow conditions to be placed on the offender, in particular the requirement that he undergoes psychiatric assessment.

To obtain a protection order, go to the front counter of your suburban magistrates' court, local court or court of petty sessions. Ask the clerk of courts or court registrar, who control the administration of the court (or in New South Wales the chamber magistrate), to help you. Ensure your street address is kept private if it is not already known to your stalker. You will be required to attend court, but in special circumstances (such as extreme fear of meeting your stalker if you appear in person) a police officer or a support worker may provide support or apply for an order on your behalf. If you have any concerns speak with the police officer assigned to your case, the court registrar or your legal adviser.

In preparing your complaint you (the 'applicant') will need to satisfy the magistrate that you have been harassed or you are the subject of stalking. If you need urgent protection, the court can make an interim order without your stalker being present. However, you will be required to attend court to explain your situation to the magistrate and why you need an order. Inform the magistrate if you believe your stalker is in possession of any firearms. The magistrate will hear the evidence and decide whether there are grounds for the order and what conditions should apply. The order will not be enforceable until it is served on the stalker by the police. Where an interim order is issued you will need to return to court in a few weeks to obtain your final order. If you do not attend your complaint will be struck out and the order will cease to exist. If the stalker has received notice of the order but fails to attend this hearing you can still proceed to obtain a final order. If you have reason to believe your safety or property is threatened, the court may issue a warrant to have the stalker arrested and brought to court for a hearing.

Occasionally, stalkers may react to an order by making a *counter* application against the victim. This causes understandable distress for many victims, who view this as a further attack on their characters. However, do not despair if the magistrate does grant a protective injunction to both parties. You are unlikely to be greatly inconvenienced as a result of the order, since you have already chosen to stay well away from your stalker. If you have been tempted to respond at various times to your stalker, thereby ultimately *encouraging* his behaviour, a court order prohibiting any contact by either party may assist in curbing these urges. There is also some research to suggest that after a protective order is issued against both parties (a 'mutual' order) victims are less likely to experience violence at the hands of their stalker (Meloy et al., 1997).

If the court decides not to make an order or you are unhappy with the terms of the order, you can appeal against this decision. You should discuss this with a lawyer. The defendant (or 'respondent') can also appeal against the issuance of the order or any of its terms. At any time during the operation of the order, either party can apply to the magistrates' court to have the order varied, revoked or extended. If you move interstate, your order can now be registered in most states of Australia without having to return to court. Check with the local court in the state or territory to which you are moving.

It is, of course, essential that an order is enforced once it is issued. It is a criminal offence to disobey the conditions of the order, and any breach must be reported to the police. The police should then make an arrest, but they may give the stalker a summons to appear in court at a later date. If he continues his harassment before the date of the court hearing, advise the police and insist that he is arrested.

Protection orders should not be regarded as a routine approach to stalking. There is no universal recommendation about their use, and you are advised to consult with appropriate professionals, such as the police, a lawyer, victims of crime support services or a mental health specialist, to determine whether such an order is likely to be of benefit given the circumstances of your case. Protection orders are generally best viewed as a useful adjunct to other legal proceedings if initiated *early* in the course of stalking. Obtaining an order should not bring with it expectations, at least in the immediate term, of protection and resolution of harassment.

Lawyers

The cost of retaining the services of a lawyer may be prohibitive for many stalking victims, but the advantage is that they know the legal system. You may apply for free legal advice through legal aid services, although they do not deal with every legal problem and many people are ineligible for free assistance. Free advice can also be obtained from your nearest Citizen's Advice Bureau or Community Legal Centre. They can also recommend the names of local lawyers who may help you. The Law Institute or Society in your state, the organization representing lawyers, can provide information as well as referral to a suitable lawyer. If you retain the services of a private lawyer first ask for a written estimate of the cost. If you cannot afford this, ask the lawyer to help you pay for assistance through legal aid, which may then fund your lawyer to take the case.

It is often useful to ask your lawyer to send the stalker a letter by certified mail, demanding that he stops stalking immediately or he will face legal action. This again gives a very clear message to all but the most disordered of stalkers, and some will stop after such a warning.

While most stalking victims are not legally represented in protection order hearings, lawyers can advise on the suitability and terms of these orders.

They can also assist you in other legal proceedings pertaining to the stalker's prosecution, advise you on applying for criminal compensation and help with any civil suit should you wish to pursue restitution against the stalker (see below).

Court

The vast majority of victims are novices within the criminal justice system. They often feel overawed at court, and this seemingly unsympathetic and formal environment may reinforce feelings of incompetence and helplessness. You can reduce your anxiety by being informed about how the criminal justice system works and your role in the process.

After you report the stalking to the police they will investigate the crime. The police officer dealing directly with the victim is known as the investigating officer or 'the informant' in court proceedings. If you need to communicate further information to the police, contact the investigating officer. Police may not be able to provide anything other than general information regarding the progress of their enquiries if this could affect the investigation.

When your stalker is charged with an offence (usually stalking or related offences) he may be interviewed and released on bail, to attend court at a later date. Alternatively, the stalker (the 'defendant' or 'accused') may be held in custody after being charged. He may remain in custody until a court hears the case or he may later be released on bail until the case is heard. Contact the investigating officer if you are concerned that the stalker's release will endanger you or your family and the police will advise the magistrate accordingly. There will be a condition on the defendant's bail that he makes no contact with you or your family.

In the first instance, the stalking allegations will be heard in a magistrates' or local court (unless the defendant was under 17 years at the time of the crimes, in which case he will usually be tried in a children's court). Magistrates' courts are the lowest in the court hierarchy and are located in many suburbs and regional centres. The case will be prosecuted by a police prosecutor and may be defended by a barrister or solicitor representing the stalker. Neither the lawyers nor the presiding magistrate (who is referred to as 'Your Worship') wear wigs or gowns.

Although most first time stalkers are currently dealt with in the magistrates' court, occasionally these cases will proceed to a higher court. This is usually because they are more serious (in legal terms e.g. involving assault with a weapon) or because an appeal has been lodged against the magistrate's decision. In these courts (the county or district court and the higher supreme court) the stalker will be tried before a judge (referred to as 'Your Honour') with or without a jury. Instead of a police prosecutor, the case will be prosecuted by a lawyer (usually a barrister acting on the instructions of the Office of Public Prosecutions). Judges and lawyers in the county court usually wear wigs and gowns.

If the defendant pleads guilty you may not need to give evidence in court, but if he pleads not guilty your testimony may be required. This can be particularly problematic in stalking cases because the victim's presence in court can gratify the stalker's need for contact. If the prospect of face-to-face contact with your stalker (and perhaps his family) in the courtroom distresses you, speak with the police prosecutor, your lawyer, if you have one, or the court's witness assistance services where these exist (see below). Application can be made to the court for consideration of alternative arrangements, such as giving evidence from a place other than the courtroom by closed circuit television or the use of screens to remove the defendant from your direct line of vision.

Courts can be rather unwelcoming places. If possible, take along a supportive friend or family member. Often courts provide professionally trained volunteer support workers or a witness assistance service for those who are unfamiliar with court procedures. This service generally includes the provision of precourt information, practical and emotional support throughout the court hearing and waiting rooms within the court complex. The police or court information desk will provide you with their contact details. It is best to arrange this service ahead of the scheduled court hearing so that someone is available for you. A support worker can show you around when the courts are not in session.

If you have special needs, give the prosecutor advance notice. Interpreters can be arranged for victims who do not speak English or those who are hearing impaired, and, if you are Aboriginal or a Torres Strait Islander, the court will arrange for support from someone who understands your culture.

After the magistrate (or judge and jury) hears the case he or she will find the defendant either guilty or not guilty (the jury is not required if the accused pleads guilty). Before sentencing the convicted stalker the magistrate or judge may request a report from a psychiatrist or psychologist. These will generally be professionals who are experienced in the assessment and management of mentally disordered offenders. Their opinion will assist the court in deciding on an appropriate disposition. For stalking, more than many crimes, it is essential that any legal sanctions handed down by the court take account of the nature of any psychiatric condition from which the stalker may be suffering, its amenability to treatment and the best means of delivering that treatment. However essential these psychiatric considerations may be, they should not take priority over you or your family's safety. If you are concerned about the disposition of your stalker, speak with your lawyer, the police prosecutor (or Crown Prosecutor in the higher Courts) or the police victim advisory service.

For most first time stalkers presenting before a magistrate, sentences entail a fine, good behaviour (peace) bond, probation (community correctional order) or a suspended sentence. Probation will often have conditions attached, such as the requirement that the offender undergoes psychiatric treatment or counselling for drug and alcohol abuse. If the convicted stalker does not comply with the conditions of his probation or similar order he will be returned to court and risk more serious penalties. An offender who breaches a suspended sentence by reoffending is likely to serve the remainder of the sentence in prison. When reporting further stalking activities to the police, remind them that the offender has been convicted of stalking and is on probation (or equivalent). Do not assume the police will have this information at their fingertips.

If your stalker receives a term of imprisonment and you wish to know his earliest release date, write to the office of the correctional services commissioner or its equivalent in your state or territory. If you specifically want to know whether he is to be granted parole, contact your state's adult parole board.

If the accused is found not guilty (that is, he is acquitted) this does not mean the magistrate, judge or jury disbelieves your story. A number of other factors can influence this decision, particularly the lack of sufficient evidence to prove to the satisfaction of the court or jury that stalking has occurred. (It should be noted that the standard of proof for criminal cases is more stringent than that for civil cases. In the former, the onus rests with the prosecution to convince the magistrate, judge or jury of the defendant's guilt *beyond reasonable doubt*. In civil cases, such as protection order hearings, the standard of proof is *on the balance of probabilities.*

Criminal injuries compensation

There are a number of different avenues by which victims of crime can receive payments or other financial assistance. The police will provide you with further information when you report stalking incidents. You can also seek advice and assistance through your local victims of crime support organisation or lawyer. Claim forms for criminal injuries compensation are available through these bodies or the magistrates' court in most jurisdictions. There may be a time limit for making claims.

If you are seeking compensation, you will need to have reported the crime(s) to the police and they will have to agree that the crime has occurred and that your injury or loss resulted from it. It is not necessary for them to have apprehended or charged the perpetrator. You must also be able to show that the crime actually caused your emotional and, in some instances, physical injuries, and the crimes compensation tribunal may seek evidence in support of this from your doctor, therapist or an independent specialist.

Some victims do not pursue crimes compensation because they feel unable to face another court appearance. In some jurisdictions the victim is not required to attend any hearing. For those who must appear in person, however, the court volunteer support service is available to assist you during these hearings also, and the magistrates presiding over crimes compensation cases are sensitive to victims of crime and attuned to their needs. You will not have to confront the perpetrator.

Depending on jurisdiction, successful claims may result in the payment of counselling sessions for you and others affected by the stalker, other medical expenses or loss of income expenses. It is recognized that the amount awarded can never adequately compensate for the suffering inflicted by a stalker, but for many victims a positive criminal injuries hearing offers validation and a sense of justice, which assists in the rehabilitation process.

Victims may instead seek restitution. That is, they can sue their stalker for emotional, physical or financial damages consequent upon being stalked. In these cases it is generally best to hire a lawyer; the Law Institute or Society can provide the names of personal injury lawyers. Legal advice and representation is costly, but if you retain the services of a lawyer who works on a 'contingent fee' basis he or she will recover payment from the sum awarded if the suit is successful.

13

Should I just disappear?

There are substantial costs in relocating and establishing a new identity, and in the vast majority of cases it is unnecessary. Moving away disrupts work, schooling and social ties. It is both emotionally and financially draining, especially if you have already invested in additional home security measures. Worst of all, your sacrifice may be in vain if the stalker pursues you to your next address, some stalkers proving more than equal to this challenge.

If you are seriously contemplating such action, first talk with your therapist, the police or your victims of crime support agency. Ask them what else could be done to avoid such drastic measures and for a realistic appraisal of your stalker's likelihood of tracking you down at your next address. Importantly, ask what measures need to be taken if you do move in order to minimize the likelihood of being found.

Stalking that arises between neighbours, when it is solely confined to that neighbourhood, is usually resolved by the victim's relocation. However, stalkers who are determined to maintain a relationship, particularly intimacy seekers and the rejected, have considerably more invested in their victims and will seldom give them up so easily. If fears for your safety dictate that relocation is the last available option you must ensure that you leave as few clues as possible to your new address.

While it is virtually impossible to erase your identity – even the best witness protection programmes do not always succeed in this – there are a number of weak links in the system that can be addressed.

• Start taking note of every document on which your name and contact details appear. Purchasing an unlisted phone number removes it from the phone directory, but it becomes public information whenever it appears on a public record. Your address appears on many publicly accessible documents, including your driver's licence, car registration, electoral roll and subscriptions, to name but a few.

- Do not give your forwarding address to anyone other than your most trusted and reliable friends and family members. This includes property agents. Be very vigilant about where you register your private phone number or home address, giving instead a post office box address or, if a legitimate street address is required by law, that of your lawyer's office.

- Apply to remove your name from the electoral roll. In Australia, you will need to contact your nearest electoral office and explain that, because you are being stalked, publication of your address could put your safety and that of your family at risk. Support your application with copies of any police reports or protection orders.

- In the USA, you can request that voter registration, like the Department of Motor Vehicles, withholds your address. However, despite this, certain exempt persons and agencies such as law enforcement, insurance companies, collection agencies, credit unions, banks, attorneys and even news media can still obtain your address. Furthermore, anyone can walk into your county recorder's office and if you own land in that county (e.g. where you live) the address will be provided. The only way to block this information is to own the property through a trust. An attorney can arrange this for you.

- In the UK you are required by law to provide accurate personal details to the local electoral registration officer, who has a duty to publish the electoral register for public scrutiny. However, in 2002 new regulations are likely to come into force whereby it will be possible to remove your name from the commercial register that is currently widely distributed. (This will be possible by ticking a box on the registration card sent to all households annually.) The remaining register will be accessible by the public but only from local council offices. It will not be available for commercial purposes, nor will the public be permitted to make copies. With the current register, entries are listed in address order, not by name, so an individual would have to know where you live to retrieve other details about you.

- If you are registered with any professional body, do not provide personal contact details. These are occasionally released in error despite the member indicating they are to remain confidential. Car registration details are now less accessible to the general public, but again it is wise to provide an acceptable alternative address (see *Protecting personal information*, Chapter 8).

In summary, moving away from your home, your family, work, school and social network is a major undertaking and one which you do not want to face more than once. Screen your paper trail of documents, anticipate and plug the leaks and be ever alert to additional weak spots. For further helpful advice in this area, refer to Schaum and Parrish (1995) and Snow (1998) in the reading guide.

14

How do I deal with the emotional impact of stalking?

Support organizations and self-help groups

Support organizations can provide emotional support, information and advice to victims, and they can refer victims to specialist treatment services when additional support is required. There are organizations specifically for stalking victims in the UK and North America, and the Internet is also a good source of information on support organizations. Try the search term 'stalking'. Appendix 1 lists the major international support organizations for stalking victims, as well as contact details for your nearest victims of crime support/assistance service. These organizations offer advice to victims of crime in general, and they can also refer you to agencies which can assist specific subgroups of stalking victims, such as domestic violence services for the victim of a 'rejected' stalker.

Your local victims of crime agency can also advise you on the availability of self-help and support groups for stalking victims in your area. You may wish to start your own – ask the victim agencies if they have the names of any stalking victims who are willing to be contacted by other victims. Speak with your local council, church or victims of crime support services about a suitable, secure venue.

Even if a regular group seems too ambitious or impractical at this stage, you may want to consider forming a peer network, which will place stalking victims in contact with each other, providing emotional support and an opportunity to exchange information and strategies. Inform victim services that you are willing for any newly referred stalking victims to be advised of the peer network. All such organizations, groups and networks convey one important message to stalking victims: *You are not alone.*

Counselling

For all victims the most useful therapy would be the disappearance of the stalker, but this may take some time to achieve. In any case, for most victims the psychological symptoms produced by stalking do not immediately subside when the harassment is brought under control. Victims may experience substantial emotional fall out over some months, and the psychological scars of their ordeals can be enduring.

Professional counselling can assist stalking victims. In Australia, counsellors most commonly have a background in psychology or psychiatry. A psychologist has a bachelor degree majoring in psychology. Psychiatrists are medical doctors who specialize in the treatment of mental illness. In the field of trauma counselling there is some overlap in the services both professions offer, but because psychologists are not medical doctors they cannot prescribe medication if this is required. Medicare will offer a rebate on psychiatric consultations but not on sessions with a private psychologist, though private health insurance may meet some of these costs. Also, criminal injuries compensation boards often award counselling expenses. To find a suitable counsellor consult your local victims of crime service, mental health service, community health clinic or general practitioner. If you are intending to apply for crimes compensation ensure your counsellor is approved by the crimes compensation assessor where applicable (see below).

In the US, a psychologist has a PhD in psychology. Therapists with masters degrees may have an MSW (Masters of Social Work), LCSW (Licensed Clinical Social Worker) or LPC (Licensed Professional Counsellor). As in Australia, there is some overlap in the services provided by these professions, but only a psychiatrist (a medical doctor) can prescribe medication. Be aware that anyone, without even so much as a high school diploma, can hang out a signboard and call him- or herself a 'therapist' in most states. Almost all insurance plans, Medicare and Medicaid will reimburse for counselling services, although managed care plans may require preauthorization. Money for counselling may also be obtained through victim/witness assistance.

In the UK, counsellors can be provided on the National Health Service. The best way to access these services is to consult your general practitioner, who will make the appropriate referral. Your doctor will also be able to determine your specific counselling needs, in particular whether you require the help of a trained therapist or a psychiatrist (medical specialist).

When making your appointment with the counsellor, be sure to inform his or her receptionist that you are a stalking victim and your details must be kept absolutely confidential.

Individual counselling can benefit stalking victims in a number of ways:

- While the stalking is ongoing, counselling focuses on ensuring that you and others who may be at risk are taking every reasonable step to protect your personal safety. Counsellors can provide understanding and emotional support, reducing feelings of isolation and alienation. They can also help you to make sense of your situation by bringing to sessions an understanding of stalkers and the ways in which they operate. They can offer an appraisal of the risks posed by your particular stalker, and provide you with strategies aimed at ending the stalking. Counsellors can also help you to access other services and advocate on your behalf if you feel too distressed or exhausted to do so.
- In addition to this more practical focus, counsellors can help victims to deal with their psychological turmoil. They will assist in managing anxiety symptoms, usually through a combination of relaxation training and other psychological therapies. They can help you to face your fear in a realistic manner, preventing you from becoming a recluse but without placing you at increased risk. You will be taught techniques for overcoming extreme anxiety, as in panic attacks, and improving sleep patterns. Therapy will also help you to deal with irrational beliefs that often develop in response to stalking (e.g. blaming yourself or feeling the rest of the world is a sinister place).
- Your therapist can also help with legal proceedings and criminal compensation hearings by providing written reports or verbal testimony.
- In some instances victims are so traumatized and disabled by their anxiety that medication is required in addition to the above measures. Medication will also need to be considered for victims who have developed symptoms of clinical depression. The usual indications are severe depressive symptoms that threaten to overwhelm the victim and which impair their capacity to participate in psychological therapies and often in life itself. Medication that combines antianxiety and antidepressant effects aims to

bring the victims' distress under control, allowing them to function and ultimately to triumph over their stalkers. If you are finding yourself increasing your consumption of alcohol, cigarettes, prescription tranquillisers such as diazepam (Valium) and sleeping tablets or even illegal substances such as marijuana it is imperative that you speak with your doctor about a safer, more effective, legal and nonaddictive option. He or she will discuss the actions and potential side effects of these medications and their suitability in your case.

- Counselling after the stalking has ceased can assist in your rehabilitation. This may entail continued treatment of anxiety and depression, restoring your self confidence and trust in others and repairing relationships damaged by the stalking. You may retain a degree of vigilance and caution in your day-to-day activities, but the therapist can help you to contain this to a manageable, if not adaptive, level. The overall goal in therapy is to enable you to emerge from your ordeal not just as a survivor but as a stronger person who will be far less vulnerable to the damaging effects of any subsequent abuses.

15

How you can assist victims of stalking

Our society is becoming increasingly aware of the fact that stalking is a crime and that it is widespread. As noted earlier, many people today will have some familiarity with stalking phenomena. Raising awareness about stalking and its many consequences has been an important advance, but now our understanding of these behaviours must inform more constructive approaches to their elimination, and to the assistance that is provided to stalking victims.

Victims of stalking often complain that instead of understanding they receive comments and 'advice' that reinforce their sense of guilt and self blame. Rather than support they experience abandonment; they fear for their safety but their pleas for help are ignored or trivialized. The following are some suggestions as to how various significant figures in the lives of stalking victims, both informal and more traditional sources of assistance and support, can have a more positive impact on the outcome. These are based on observations in clinical practice and the comments of victims themselves. It is not intended to be an exhaustive doctrine and the reader is referred to earlier chapters and to the reading guide at the end of this book for more detailed information relating to stalking and its effects on its victims.

Family and friends

If you too are being threatened or are otherwise at risk from the stalker make sure you have taken every reasonable step to secure your safety. While it is not unusual to feel annoyed that your loved one (hereafter termed the 'primary victim') has involved you in this and that you therefore have a right to insist that she *fixes* the problem, this reaction is not helpful. Stalking victims are not to blame, although *they* may, as part of their trauma response, experience irrational feelings of self blame. They will be exquisitely sensitive to any hint of blame from others, especially those whose opinions matter to them. Telling them what they should have done, or should be doing, implies they have acted in an irresponsible or negligent manner – that they have not or are not doing enough. The 'obvious' solutions may not be so clear to a person who is weary or befuddled by a stalker's repeated intrusions or they may already have been tried to no effect. Some victims simply try so hard and hit so many brick walls that they eventually give up.

The family and friends of stalking victims quite often feel helpless. Their commonsense solutions repeatedly fail, leaving them with a loved one whose suffering defies any fast or reliable cure. It may be tempting to withdraw from the victim to avoid being continually confronted by your apparent ineffectuality, but resist this inclination at all costs. *Do not give up on your loved one because you are unable to fix her problem.* She needs your emotional support and somebody she can trust. She does not want to have to do this alone. So often, victims of stalking say that they have lost all their friends and that their families are sick of them. This is seldom the case, but it may well be their interpretation of the situation.

It is often helpful to ask the primary victim *what she needs from you.* She may request practical help (e.g. being alert to suspicious activity around the house) or ask you to be available to talk. Talking can be an emotional drain, and you may want to consider helping the primary victim to join or set up a support group or peer network (see Chapter 14).

Living with a stalking victim is not easy. Some victims appear to undergo a personality change. Repeated, unpredictable trauma like stalking can have a major impact on one's psychological and physical functioning. Familiarize yourself with the reactions to extreme stress outlined in Chapter 7. If you are concerned for the primary victim's mental or physical health, try to encourage her to seek professional help (see Chapter 14), or ask someone in a position of influence to do this. Offer to escort her to her appointment.

This will be a testing time. Do not underestimate your role in it. The victim needs a buttress to weather the stalker's gale force gusts. You may not be able to eradicate the problem, but with your unwavering support your loved one will survive.

Employers and co-workers

The above principles also apply to the employers and work colleagues of stalking victims. Employers have a responsibility to protect workers from harassment and violence in the workplace. Indeed, an employer who fails to take appropriate action when one employee stalks or harasses another can be sued for monetary damages by the victim for fostering a 'hostile work environment'. Review safety protocols and arrange for any additional security measures such as out of hours escorts for the primary victim. If the stalker is also an employee he must be dealt with swiftly and assertively. Failure to observe distinct instructions from a senior level to refrain from harassing behaviours must have clearly stated consequences – at the very least, transfer or termination from the victim's workplace. Employers who fail in their obligation to take affirmative action are likely to lose the stalked employee and at some point find themselves confronting further victimization of another innocent employee. Tragedies have occurred in workplaces around the world because employers, for whatever reason, neglected to act in the face of stalking in their workplace.

The victim's work performance may be impaired as a consequence of traumatic stress symptoms, and her attendance may be affected by fear of travel or the competing demands of court hearings, doctor's appointments and attendances at police stations. This can create an added burden for fellow workers, resulting in frustration and marginalization of the victim. Employers can improve the morale and safety of all workers and minimize further trauma to the victim by ensuring staff are properly informed and by involving the victim and relevant co-workers in developing a safety plan.

If the stalked worker is clearly no longer capable of performing even light duties she should be encouraged to seek professional help. She may need help to arrange sick leave and workers' compensation benefits where eligible. Some employees receiving workers' compensation for stress symptoms induced by stalking experience the bureaucracy and requirements of workers' compensation as intrusive and revictimizing. It is often beneficial to appoint a suitable contact person in the workplace to assist the victim and minimize the bureaucratic demands on her.

Police

While some stalking victims are satisfied with the manner in which their case has been handled by the police, others are more critical. One of the main complaints is the failure of police to take victims' concerns seriously. Victims also complain about the apparent unfamiliarity of police with stalking legislation and their failure to enforce protection orders and stalking laws properly. Even without any additional resources there is much that can be done by some sectors of law enforcement to minimize the distress and damage inflicted by stalkers on their victims.

Ensure stalking victims, as for any victims of crime, are provided with information on victim's rights and appropriate support services. In cases where the stalker is charged, inform the victim of the prosecution process, and endeavour to notify her of the hearing date whether or not her presence in court is required. Advise her if the proceedings are discontinued and the reason for this. Perhaps more than many crime victims who may have suffered a single assault, stalking victims who remain vulnerable to *continuing* harassment are anxious to learn the outcome of the proceedings.

Clearly, police need to be familiar with the wording of the stalking legislation in their jurisdiction. In those instances where the legal criteria are fulfilled it may, for a variety of reasons, be more appropriate in the first instance to charge the offender with stalking than to recommend that the victim applies for a protection order (see Chapter 10).

In addition to keeping abreast of relevant legislation, police officers would benefit from an understanding of the behaviours that constitute stalking, the perpetrators of these behaviours, the motivations underlying them and the impact of stalking on victims. This should be included in the training curricula of new recruits and operational officers. A working knowledge of stalker characteristics will improve the chances of apprehending them at the earliest juncture and facilitate appropriate intervention. Insight into the effects of stalking will foster a more productive relationship with the victim and involved third parties, and it is likely to defuse distress rather than exacerbate it.

While it may be reasonable to reassure some stalking victims, do not trivialize their complaints. Realistic risk appraisals can be made only when all the details of the case are available. If this is the first time you have dealt with the victim, do not dismiss the complainant's report of trampled garden plants as unworthy of further action because it may well be preceded by 20 other incident reports showing a clear 'course of conduct'. Chapter 4 highlighted those stalking situations that pose greater risk to the victim's physical integrity. In these cases especially, delaying action while awaiting the requisite number of incidents by law is obviously unacceptable to most victims and vulnerable third parties. An appreciation of the factors associated with a heightened risk of violence and those stalkers who are likely to pose the greatest threat is critical to timely intervention *before* the victim is emotionally or physically incapacitated, or worse.

Victims who express satisfaction with the police response are generally those who were assigned a dedicated officer (or two). Because these officers have a thorough understanding of the case, the victim is spared the trauma and inefficiency of repeating the story to yet another stranger every time she needs to report an incident. The police concerned can also build a better overall picture of the stalker, his patterns of harassment and the risk posed to the victim. They will be in a far better position to advise the victims on their options with respect to intervention and can be a trusted source of information and support in any subsequent legal proceedings.

Police should respond to stalking victims not only with thoroughness but with compassion and sensitivity as well. Victims may be distraught and the harassment they report occasionally borders on the bizarre, but this is seldom an indication that the victim is mad or hysterical or malingering. While some individuals with paranoid psychotic illnesses can experience delusions that they are being stalked, these cases are relatively uncommon and in most instances can be readily discerned by their implausible, inconsistent and often bizarre nature (e.g. that the stalker is entering their home through the walls at night and sexually molesting them as they sleep). Other clues are the deluded victim's belief that *many* stalkers are involved or claims of one ringleader who has involved an entire network of people to monitor and menace the victim. These 'victims' generally cannot offer an adequate or logical explanation for the ludicrous lengths to which their conspirators are prepared to go. What is clear, however, is that they suffer no less than true stalking victims, since they genuinely believe in their persecution. They have no intention of wasting police time and resources, and they seek no rewards other than the elimination of the imagined stalker(s). Charging such individuals with making false reports may deter them from approaching the police, but it will not extinguish their delusions and fears (some incorporating the police into the conspiracy). These individuals are often isolated in the first place (a risk factor for the development of these disorders) and unlikely as a consequence of their poor insight to seek psychiatric help; some will resort to taking their own action to protect themselves. This may have disastrous consequences for the innocent people who are perceived to be their persecutors. Deluded victims, or those in whom police suspect major mental illness in the absence of objective evidence of stalking, should be discussed with local mental health services to establish the need for psychiatric assessment and a strategy to effect this.

Finally, and importantly, do not caution stalkers or recommend that the victim takes out a protection order unless you intend to follow through with the necessary action in the event that the warning or order is breached. A lack of affirmative action gives a distinct message to stalkers that their activities will be tolerated and that the behaviour is not considered by the law to be problematic. Inaction may even reinforce an offender's belief that the *victim* is the problem and that the police are sympathetic to the stalker. Equally damaging is the message conveyed to victims when the law is not enforced. They feel their suffering has not been taken seriously, that the police have betrayed them and that the 'system' can no longer be relied upon to protect them. Feelings of helplessness and isolation are exacerbated, and in some cases suicide becomes a serious consideration. At best, the unsupported stalking victim is susceptible to the development of serious traumatic stress symptoms that can produce long-term social, psychological and vocational disability.

Magistrates and judges

Few stalking victims choose to attend court. As for any victim of crime, the prospect of meeting the perpetrator evokes fear and anxiety. However, for some *stalking* victims the crime is ongoing and this encounter in the courtroom facilitates the unwanted contact rather than bringing about its closure.

Magistrates who preside over protection order hearings or stalking prosecutions can amplify the distress of victims through a failure to appreciate the effects of stalking on the lives of victims and their families or the dynamics of stalking, particularly a stalker's need for proximity to the object of his attentions. The earlier chapters in this book provide a useful summary of the pathology and motives of stalkers and the impact of their behaviours on those they target.

It is not unusual for stalkers to respond to a protection order by applying for an injunction against their *victims,* alleging it is they who are being harassed. While in most cases this is a wilful fabrication motivated by revenge or the desire for further contact, however adversarial, some stalkers do actually view themselves as the victim. Magistrates presiding over cross applications, in which both parties claim to be the victim in the matter, must determine who is the primary offender. This will obviously be based on the objective evidence and not on gender or other stereotypes. Be aware that some stalkers are quite intelligent, plausible and even charismatic and this may contrast sharply with the seemingly less rational, less organized, emotionally unstable presentation of the traumatized victim. In some cases, it may be necessary to issue protective orders to both parties. The true stalking victim will probably be little inconvenienced by not having contact with her stalker, while the stalker may feel less humiliation and rage at the victim if she is just as restrained as he is. In these circumstances he may pose less of a threat to his victim (Meloy et al., 1997).

If stalkers cannot be prevented from exercising their civil rights to further judicial hearings, magistrates and judges should at least consider alternative arrangements for hearing the victim's evidence, such as allowing the victim to give evidence from a separate room via closed circuit television or using screens in the courtroom. This will minimize the level of contact between stalker and victim and the gratification experienced by the stalker. It will also greatly diminish the victim's anxiety.

Some magistrates have felt rather perturbed by the courtroom behaviour of distraught victims. Indeed, so called 'hysterical' victims are occasionally referred by the court for psychiatric assessment, while clearly disturbed stalkers are not extended this consideration. An understanding of the impact of repeated and protracted harassment, especially the characteristic psychological sequelae, may pave the way for more sensitive and constructive handling of stalking victims in court. It is appropriate, however, to refer victims for counselling or for the court to provide information regarding the availability of these services for victims. In many cases, this may be the best means of establishing control over the stalker.

An understanding of the effects of stalking will also help magistrates and judges to appreciate the fear engendered in grown men by petite female stalkers or in men or women pursued by individuals who express undying love rather than death threats. It may diminish any prejudices surrounding stalking that has arisen in the context of an actual relationship and in instances where the protagonists are of the same gender.

If there are recesses that require the victim to remain at the courthouse be mindful of their safety. They should have somewhere to wait that is secure and separate from their stalkers. Court security staff, court support workers or court mental health services need to be advised of the situation.

Psychiatric assessment of convicted stalkers enables more informed sentencing. These assessments are especially useful in cases where the stalker is found to have a mental illness or other disorder that is amenable to psychiatric intervention, though practical recommendations can often be made even in the absence of such disorders. Few stalkers, however, acknowledge any need for therapy. It is therefore critical that noncustodial sentences facilitate intervention by including psychiatric assessment/treatment conditions and that the sentence is of sufficient duration to enable the referral and assessment to occur and for treatment to be initiated. Without a treatment mandate, in most cases the stalker is likely to continue offending, other legal sanctions notwithstanding, placing the victim and others at risk.

Conclusions

It is encouraging to see the attention that this relatively new category of offending is receiving from law makers, law enforcers, academics and health professionals alike. Nonetheless, as many readers will attest, there is much scope for improvement in the way we tackle this menace to society. In order for you to fight back effectively you must:

- Try to understand what you are up against. Be informed about stalking.
- Develop a strategic plan. Involve others as appropriate, ensuring top priority is given to the safety of all concerned.
- Be aware of your rights as a victim.
- Have an appreciation of the criminal justice process and your role in it.
- Be acquainted with the services best qualified to assist you, and know how to make optimal use of these.

It is hoped that this book, through its attention to these important areas, has invested you and your supports with the power to stop the stalking and to make the transition from victim to strategist and ultimately to *survivor*.

References

American Psychiatric Association. (1994). *Diagnostic and statistical manual of mental disorders.* Washington, DC: American Psychiatric Association.

Australian Bureau of Statistics. (1996). *Women's safety.* Canberra, Australia: Government Printer.

Budd, T. and Mattinson, J. (2000). *The extent and nature of stalking: Findings from the 1998 British Crime Survey.* London: Home Office Research, Development and Statistics Directorate.

Meloy, J.R., Cowett, P.Y., Parker, S.B., Hofland, B. and Friedland, A. (1997). Domestic protection orders and the prediction of subsequent criminality and violence toward protectees. *Psychotherapy*, **34**(4), 447-58.

Mudge, T. (2001). Warning – secure your data. *Australian Medicine*, 19 March, 13.

Mullen, P.E., Pathé, M., Purcell, R. and Stuart, G.W. (1999). Study of stalkers. *American Journal of Psychiatry* **156**, 1244–9.

Pathé, M. and Mullen, P.E. (1997). The impact of stalkers on their victims. *British Journal of Psychiatry*, **170**, 12–17.

Pathé, M., Mullen, P.E. and Purcell, R. (2000). Same gender stalkers. *Journal of the American Academy of Psychiatry and the Law*, **28**, 191–7

Purcell, R., Pathé, M. and Mullen, P.E. (2002). The prevalence and nature of stalking in the Australian community. *Australian and New Zealand Journal of Psychiatry*, **36**, 114–20.

Tjaden, P. and Thoennes, N. (1998). *Stalking in America: Findings from the National Violence Against Women Survey: Research in brief.* Washington, DC: National Institute of Justice Centers for Disease Control and Prevention.

United Kingdom only

Brown H. (2000). *Stalking and other forms of harassment: An investigators guide.* London: Metropolitan Police Service (http://www.met.police/stalking/guide.htm)

Harris, J. (2000). *An evaluation of the use and effectiveness of the Protection from Harassment Act 1997.* Home Office Research Study no 203. London: Home Office.

137

Reading guide

Books

Allen, J.G. (1995). *Coping With trauma: a guide to self-understanding.* Washington, DC: American Psychiatric Press.

> A useful resource for trauma victims and their families. While not specific to stalking victims, it gives good coverage of the effects of trauma such as stalking, and discusses trauma related psychiatric disorders and their treatment.

de Becker, G. (1997). *The gift of fear: Survival signals that protect us from violence.* London: Bloomsbury.

> An easy-to-read, commonsense guide for people concerned for their safety and that of their families. American security expert Gavin de Becker evaluates threats and provides advice to prominent media figures, corporations, law enforcement agencies and ordinary citizens including stalking victims.

Fine, R. (1997). *Being stalked: A memoir.* London: Chatto and Windus.

> An astonishing first-person account of a university lecturer in the UK pursued by a disturbed female student and her family, and his struggle to obtain justice.

Gross, L. (2000). *Surviving a stalker.* New York: Marlowe & Company.

> Originally published in 1994 under the title *To Have or To Harm*, this book provides interesting true stories in a well written and readable form. The chapter on safety strategies is particularly useful.

Meloy, J.R. (ed.). (1998). *The psychology of stalking: Clinical and forensic perspectives.* San Diego: Academic Press.

> With scholarly contributions from a range of authors, this book explores stalking from social, psychiatric, psychological, legal and behavioural perspectives. The chapter on victims by Doris M Hall is based on her North American survey of 145 victims of stalking.

Mullen, P.E., Pathé, M. and Purcell, R. (2000). *Stalkers and their victims.* Cambridge, UK:Cambridge University Press.

> A comprehensive book by Australian authors that provides detailed coverage of stalking and its impact. It has a strong clinical focus, the authors having many years' collective experience in assessing and treating stalkers and stalking victims. It contains numerous case descriptions.

Orion, D. (1997). *I know you really love me: A psychiatrist's journal of erotomania, stalking, and obsessive love.* New York: Macmillan.

> A vivid portrayal of a psychiatrist's struggle to overcome the attentions of a former patient. This is particularly relevant to health professionals who are stalked by their patients, victims of same gender stalking and victims of erotomanic stalkers. It highlights the shortcomings of the criminal justice system for stalking victims in the USA.

Schaum, M. and Parrish, K. (1995). *Stalked: Breaking the silence on the crime of stalking in America.* New York: Pocket Books.

> This is a comprehensive guide for stalking victims, containing case studies, interviews with stalking victims, advocates, psychologists, and legal and security experts. It features a range of practical strategies for victims, not all of which have applicability outside North America.

Snow, R.L. (1998). *Stopping a stalker: A cop's guide to making the system work for you.* New York: Plenum Trade.

> Captain Snow draws upon 25 years in the police force to provide his views on the crime of stalking and advice to stalking victims on how best to protect themselves. This book is a useful resource for victims negotiating the legal system, but it is of less relevance to victims outside the United States. There is an abundance of case material.

(United Kingdom only)

Infield, P. and Platford, G. (2000). *The law of harassment and stalking.* London: Butterworths.
> A detailed and practical guide to the Protection from Harassment Act 1997, written by two barristers. While it is aimed mainly at lawyers and police, it offers victims a greater understanding of this complex legal area.

Journal articles

Deirmenjian, J.M. (1999). Stalking in cyberspace. *Journal of the American Academy of Psychiatry and the Law,* **27**(3), 407–13.

Mullen, P.E., Pathé, M., Purcell, R. and Stuart, G.W. (1999). Study of stalkers. *American Journal of Psychiatry,* **156**, 1244–9.

Pathé, M. and Mullen, P.E. (1997). The impact of stalkers on their victims. *British Journal of Psychiatry,* **170**, 12–17.

Pathé, M., Mullen, P.E. and Purcell, R. (2000). Same-gender stalking. *Journal of the American Academy of Psychiatry and the Law,* **28**, 191–7.

Purcell, R., Pathé, M. and Mullen, P.E. (in press). Stalking: defining and prosecuting a new form of offending. *International Journal of Law and Psychiatry.*

(United Kingdom only)

Harris, J. (2000). *An evaluation of the use and effectiveness of the Protection from Harassment Act 1997.* Home Office Research Study no 203. London: Home Office.

Appendix 1: Other resources

United States

Communities Against Violence Network (CAVNET)

www.cavnet.org

The Stalking Assistance Site

www.stalkingassistance.com

A comprehensive, practical resource designed by women with over 20 years' combined experience in federal law enforcement and threat management. Step-by-step detailed instruction is provided in a variety of relevant areas. Professional consulting services are donated at a reduced rate by a highly experienced threat assessment and management consultant and a 900 telephone number is additionally offered as another option for immediate support.

Information for stalking victims

www.antistalking.com

National Criminal Justice Reference Service

www.ncjrs.org

P.O. Box 6000

Rockville, MD 20849-6000

(800) 851-3420

Sponsored by the National Institute of Justice. Provides reports on various studies conducted by the Institute on stalking, violence and domestic abuse.

National Organization for Victim Assistance (NOVA)

1757 Park Rd., NW

Washington, DC 20010

(800) 879-6682 or (202) 232-6682

A free 24-hour victim hotline providing information and referral to resources in the victim's own state.

Survivors of Stalking (S.O.S.)
> www.soshelp.org
> PO Box 20762
> Tampa, Florida 33622
> Telephone 1-813-889-0767
> Provides workshops on stalking. Victims and others can also order cassettes of these workshops, which include information on stalking, laws, threat assessment, safety and workplace violence. Lists support groups for victims in various states and provides information, support and referral.

The Stalking Victims Sanctuary
> www.stalkingvictims.com

National Center for Victims of Crime
> www.ncvc.org
> 2111 Wilson Blvd., Suite 300
> Arlington, VA 22201
> (703) 276-2880
> Through Infolink, (800) FYI-CALL or (817) 877-3355, victims and others may obtain information and referral on victim and crime-related issues. Open Mon-Fri 9am-5.30pm.

National Victim Center stalking law fact sheets
> http://aspensys.aspensys.com:209/R0-185754-range/ncjrs/data/anticode.txt and
> http://www.nvc.org/ddir/info71.htm

National Victim Center help guide for stalking victims
> http://www.ojp.usdoj.gov/ovc/assist/nvaa/ch21-2st.htm

National Victim Center safety tips
> http://www.ojp.usdoj.gov/ovc/help/stalk/info44.htm

State stalking laws
> http://www.nvc.org/gdir/svsafety.htm

Privacy Rights Clearing House
> http://www.privacyrights.org

National Domestic Violence Hotline

3616 Far West Blvd., Suite 101-297

Austin, TX 87831

(800) 799-7233

A free, 24-hour hotline that provides victims with referrals to agencies in their local area.

Canada

Canadian Resource Center for Victims of Crime

141 Catherine Street, Suite 100

Ottawa, Ontario K2P 1C3

(613) 233-7614

Information and assistance to victims and their families with respect to sentence administration, parole authorities and securing legal counsel.

Victims for Justice

PO Box 22023

3079 Forestglade Drive

Windsor, Ontario N8R 2H5

(519) 972-0836

An organization that provides a research library of stalking incidents in Canada as well as handouts on *How to Survive a Stalker* and *How to Safeguard Yourself.*

Barbara Schilfer Commemorative Clinic

489 College Street, Suite 503

Toronto, Ontario M6G 1A5

(416) 323-9149

Provides free legal, counselling, cultural interpretation and information and referral services to women who are survivors of violence.

Australia

(Note also websites listed above)

Victim services		
Victoria	Stalking and Threat Management Centre	PO Box 2144 Royal Melbourne Hospital Victoria 3050 Ph (03) 9349 5477
New South Wales	Victims of Crime Bureau	Level 6, 299 Elizabeth Street Sydney NSW 2000 Telephone (02) 9374 3000 or 1800 633 063 (country areas)
New South Wales	Victims of Crime Assistance League (VOCAL)	Telephone (02) 9743 1636 (Sydney) Telephone (02) 9426 5826 (Newcastle)
Queensland	Victims of Crime Association	5 Croydon Road, Woodridge Queensland 4114 Telephone (07) 3290 2513 (Brisbane Office) Telephone 1300 73 3777 (24 h)
South Australia	Victim Support Service	11 Halifax Street Adelaide SA 5000 Telephone (08) 8231 5626 or 1800 182 368 (country)
Western Australia	Assisting Victims of Crime	6th Floor, 81 St George's Terrace Perth WA 6000 Telephone (09) 322 3711 (metro) 1800 818 988 (country)
Tasmania	Victims of Crime Service	160 New Town Road, New Town, Tasmania 7008 Telephone (03) 6228 7628
Australian Capital Territory	Victims of Crime Assistance League (VOCAL)	1 Iluka Street, Narrabundah, ACT 2604 Telephone (02) 6295 9600
Northern Territory	Victims of Crime Assistance League (VOCAL)	43 Mitchell Street, Darwin, NT 0800 Telephone 1800 672 242 (24h)

United Kingdom

Network for Surviving Stalking	A national organization providing a range of support to those affected by stalking	01344 773832
Suzy Lamplugh Trust	National charity working to promote personal safety and a safer society	14 East Sheen Avenue, London SW14 8AS 0208 876 0305
Women's Aid Federation	Free support, advice and information on refuges for women suffering from domestic abuse	0345 023468
Malicious Phone Calls	British Telecom offer free advice and a leaflet	0800 666700 for recorded message. Dial 150 free 8am-6pm Mon-Sat
Social Services	If you and your children need to escape a violent partner, Social Services can put you in touch with local refuges for women	Local Social Services Department
Rape Crisis	Sympathetic support and advice	For nearest centre call 02078371000 In Scotland call 0131 556 9437
Citizen's Advice Bureau	Where to obtain free legal advice	Local phone book/public library
CrimeStoppers	UK charity that provides an anonymous free hotline for the reporting of crimes	0800 555 111

Crime Prevention websites	
Guide to crime prevention	Advice and information from the Home Office on crime reduction, personal safety advice, support http://www.homeoffice.gov.uk/crimprev/cpindex.htm
Neighbourhood Watch	Reduce crime locally by getting together with neighbours http://www.homeoffice.gov.uk/crimprev/cpnw.htm
Personal safety	Precautions which can reduce your risk of attack http://www.homeoffice.gov.uk/crimprev/personalsafety.htm
Suzy Lamplugh Trust	A charity for personal safety and a safer society http://www.suzylamplugh.org/
Household security	Beat the burglar: make your home more secure http://www.homeoffice.gov.uk/crimprev/cpbtb.htm
Peace of mind when you are away	4 out of 5 burglaries occur when you house or flat is empty. Don't advertise you are away http://www.homeoffice.gov.uk/crimprev/gs_index.htm
Postcoding property	Mark property to deter burglars and help police http://www.homeoffice.gov.uk/crimprev/cpck.htm
Crime Stoppers	A charity partnership between police, media and community to fight crime http://www.crimestoppers-uk.org/index2.asp
Security systems	National Approval Council for Security Systems. Recognises, inspects and regulates firms who install, maintain and monitor electronic security systems http://www.nacoss.org/welcome2.htm
Locksmiths	Master Locksmiths Association: guidelines on minimum security requirements and how to find a locksmith http://www.locksmiths.co.uk/trade_division/guidelines http://www.locksmiths.co.uk/trade_division/map.htm
Police	Official police forces on website of police Information Technology Organisation (PITO) http://www.police.uk/

Information websites

Crime Statistics	Get the latest crime figures from the Home Office http://www.homeoffice.gov.uk/rds/index.htm
Stalking figures	The extent and nature of stalking: findings from the 1998 British Crime Survey http://www.homeoffice.gov.uk/rds/pdfs/hors210.pdf
Crime	This site offers links to many crime related sites http://www.ukonline.gov.uk
Victims of crime	What happens when you report a crime to police. Information on investigations, courts, compensation, help and advice http://www.homeoffice.gov.uk/cpd/pvu/pvu.htm
Effectiveness of Protection from Harassment Act 1997	Research Findings from the Protection of Harassment Act 1997: an evaluation of its use and effectiveness http://www.homeoffice.gov.uk/rds/pdfs/r130.pdf
Criminal Justice System	Gateway to the criminal justice system http://www.criminal-justice-system.gov.uk/
Crown Prosecution Service	Information about the role of the CPS http://www.cps.gov.uk/
Courts	Court Service website http://www.courtservice.gov.uk/
Scottish Courts	Scottish Courts Website http://www.scotcourts.gov.uk/
Witness in court	Information on what to expect when giving evidence in court http://www.homeoffice.gov.uk/cpd/pvu/witness.pdf
Probation	Inner London Probation Service: many useful links to other services http://www.ilps.demon.co.uk/
Prisons	Prison Service website http://www.hmprisonservice.gov.uk/
Release of prisoners	This explains the circumstances in which the Probation Service will advise you of an offender's movements after he is sent to prison http://www.homeoffice.gov.uk/cpd/pvu/ropeng.pdf
Lord Chancellor's Department	Government department for administration of justice http://www.lcd.gov.uk/lcdhome.htm
Stalking victims	General advice for stalking victims. Provides access to an investigator's guide (how police deal with stalking cases) http://www.met.police/stalking/guide.htm

Help, support, advice websites

Police	Online notification of nonurgent minor crime http://www.online.police.uk/english/default.asp
Local police station	Contact local police station in nonurgent situations http://www.police.uk/
Citizens Advice Bureau	Information on rights, gives a broad outline of where you stand and what you can do http://www.nacab.org.uk/ http://www.adviceguide.org.uk
Samaritans	A registered charity providing emotional support to those who are despairing or suicidal http://www.samaritans.org
Women's Aid	A key national charity in England for women and children experiencing physical, sexual or emotional abuse at home http://www.womensaid.org.uk
Victims	This site offers some useful leaflets http://www.homeoffice.gov.uk/cpd/pvu/vicuse.htm
Victim Support	An independent registered charity. Offers help, support and advice to victims of crime http://www.victimsupport.com
Victims Charter	This charter explains the standard of service you should expect after reporting a crime http://www.homeoffice.gov.uk/cpd/pvu/viccont.htm
Medical	To search for local medical services or advice on health matters (or call 0845 4647) http://www.nhsdirect.nhs.uk

Legal advice websites

Legal Services Commission	A public body to run the community legal service and the criminal defence service http://www.legalservices.gov.uk/
Community Legal Service	For those who need information on a legal problem. Provides legal advice or help to find legal advice. http://www.justask.gov.uk/
Legal Advice	This site gives details of over 15 000 solicitors and advice agencies. http://www.justask.org.uk/public/en/directory

Legal advice websites—*cont.*	
Compensation	Criminal Injuries Compensation Authority: explains how to apply for compensation http://www.cica.gov.uk/
Complaints	What to do if you are unhappy about the way you have been treated http://www.homeoffice.gov.uk/viccomp.htm
Law Society	The official website of the professional body for solicitors in England and Wales http://www.lawsoc.org.uk/home.asp

Assistance for victims of cyberstalking

CyberAngels

http://www.cyberangels.org

Online Harassment Resources

http://www.io.com/~barton/harassment.html

Women Take Back the Net

http://www.virtual.net/Projects/Take-Back-the-Net/

Privacy In Cyberspace

http://www.privacyrights.org/fs/fs18-cyb.html

Gender Harassment on the Internet

http://www.gsu.edu/~lawppw/lawand.papers/harass.html

Working to Halt Online Abuse

www.haltabuse.org

Love Me Not

www.lovemenot.org
Established by the Los Angeles District Attorney's Office

Appendix 2: Protection from Harassment Act 1997

Protection from Harassment Act 1997

1997 Chapter 40

An Act to make provision for protecting persons from harassment and similar conduct.

[21st March 1997]

BE IT ENACTED by the Queen's most Excellent Majesty, by and with the advice and consent of the Lords Spiritual and Temporal, and Commons, in this present Parliament assembled, and by the authority of the same, as follows:-

England and Wales

Prohibition of harassment.

1. –
   (1) A person must not pursue a course of conduct–
      (a) which amounts to harassment of another, and
      (b) which he knows or ought to know amounts to harassment of the other.
   (2) For the purposes of this section, the person whose course of conduct is in question ought to know that it amounts to harassment of another if a reasonable person in possession of the same information would think the course of conduct amounted to harassment of the other.
   (3) Subsection (1) does not apply to a course of conduct if the person who pursued it shows–
      (a) that it was pursued for the purpose of preventing or detecting crime,
      (b) that it was pursued under any enactment or rule of law or to comply with any condition or requirement imposed by any person under any enactment, or
      (c) that in the particular circumstances the pursuit of the course of conduct was reasonable.

Offence of harassment.

2. –

(1) A person who pursues a course of conduct in breach of section 1 is guilty of an offence.

(2) A person guilty of an offence under this section is liable on summary conviction to imprisonment for a term not exceeding six months, or a fine not exceeding level 5 on the standard scale, or both.

(3) In section 24(2) of the Police and Criminal Evidence Act 1984 (arrestable offences), after paragraph (m) there is inserted – "(n) an offence under section 2 of the Protection from Harassment Act 1997 (harassment).".

Civil remedy

3. –

(1) An actual or apprehended breach of section 1 may be the subject of a claim in civil proceedings by the person who is or may be the victim of the course of conduct in question.

(2) On such a claim, damages may be awarded for (among other things) any anxiety caused by the harassment and any financial loss resulting from the harassment.

(3) Where –

(a) in such proceedings the High Court or a county court grants an injunction for the purpose of restraining the defendant from pursuing any conduct which amounts to harassment, and

(b) the plaintiff considers that the defendant has done anything which he is prohibited from doing by the injunction, the plaintiff may apply for the issue of a warrant for the arrest of the defendant.

(4) An application under subsection (3) may be made-

(a) where the injunction was granted by the High Court, to a judge of that court, and

(b) where the injunction was granted by a county court, to a judge or district judge of that or any other county court.

(5) The judge or district judge to whom an application under subsection (3) is made may only issue a warrant if-

(a) the application is substantiated on oath, and

(b) the judge or district judge has reasonable grounds for believing that the defendant has done anything which he is prohibited from doing by the injunction.

(6) Where –

(a) the High Court or a county court grants an injunction for the purpose mentioned in subsection (3)(a), and

(b) without reasonable excuse the defendant does anything which he is prohibited from doing by the injunction, he is guilty of an offence.

(7) Where a person is convicted of an offence under subsection (6) in respect of any conduct, that conduct is not punishable as a contempt of court.

(8) A person cannot be convicted of an offence under subsection (6) in respect of any conduct which has been punished as a contempt of court.

(9) A person guilty of an offence under subsection (6) is liable –

    (a) on conviction on indictment, to imprisonment for a term not exceeding five years, or a fine, or both, or

    (b) on summary conviction, to imprisonment for a term not exceeding six months, or a fine not exceeding the statutory maximum, or both.

Putting people in fear of violence.

4. –

(1) A person whose course of conduct causes another to fear, on at least two occasions, that violence will be used against him is guilty of an offence if he knows or ought to know that his course of conduct will cause the other so to fear on each of those occasions.

(2) For the purposes of this section, the person whose course of conduct is in question ought to know that it will cause another to fear that violence will be used against him on any occasion if a reasonable person in possession of the same information would think the course of conduct would cause the other so to fear on that occasion.

(3) It is a defence for a person charged with an offence under this section to show that-

    (a) his course of conduct was pursued for the purpose of preventing or detecting crime,

    (b) his course of conduct was pursued under any enactment or rule of law or to comply with any condition or requirement imposed by any person under any enactment, or

    (c) the pursuit of his course of conduct was reasonable for the protection of himself or another or for the protection of his or another's property.

(4) A person guilty of an offence under this section is liable-

    (a) on conviction on indictment, to imprisonment for a term not exceeding five years, or a fine, or both, or

    (b) on summary conviction, to imprisonment for a term not exceeding six months, or a fine not exceeding the statutory maximum, or both.

(5) If on the trial on indictment of a person charged with an offence under this section the jury find him not guilty of the offence charged, they may find him guilty of an offence under section 2.

(6) The Crown Court has the same powers and duties in relation to a person who is by virtue of subsection (5) convicted before it of an offence under section 2 as a magistrates' court would have on convicting him of the offence.

Restraining orders.

5. –

(1) A court sentencing or otherwise dealing with a person ("the defendant") convicted of an offence under section 2 or 4 may (as well as sentencing him or dealing with him in any other way) make an order under this section.

(2) The order may, for the purpose of protecting the victim of the offence, or any other person mentioned in the order, from further conduct which-

(a) amounts to harassment, or

(b) will cause a fear of violence, prohibit the defendant from doing anything described in the order.

(3) The order may have effect for a specified period or until further order.

(4) The prosecutor, the defendant or any other person mentioned in the order may apply to the court which made the order for it to be varied or discharged by a further order.

(5) If without reasonable excuse the defendant does anything which he is prohibited from doing by an order under this section, he is guilty of an offence.

(6) A person guilty of an offence under this section is liable-

(a) on conviction on indictment, to imprisonment for a term not exceeding five years, or a fine, or both, or

(b) on summary conviction, to imprisonment for a term not exceeding six months, or a fine not exceeding the statutory maximum, or both.

Limitation.

6. In section 11 of the Limitation Act 1980 (special time limit for actions in respect of personal injuries), after subsection (1) there is inserted-

"(1A) This section does not apply to any action brought for damages under section 3 of the Protection from Harassment Act 1997."

Interpretation of this group of sections.

7. –

(1) This section applies for the interpretation of sections 1 to 5.

(2) References to harassing a person include alarming the person or causing the person distress.

(3) A "course of conduct" must involve conduct on at least two occasions.

(4) "Conduct" includes speech.

Scotland

Harassment.

8. –

(1) Every individual has a right to be free from harassment and, accordingly, a person must not pursue a course of conduct which amounts to harassment of another and-

    (a) is intended to amount to harassment of that person; or

    (b) occurs in circumstances where it would appear to a reasonable person that it would amount to harassment of that person.

(2) An actual or apprehended breach of subsection (1) may be the subject of a claim in civil proceedings by the person who is or may be the victim of the course of conduct in question; and any such claim shall be known as an action of harassment.

(3) For the purposes of this section-

"conduct" includes speech;

"harassment" of a person includes causing the person alarm or distress; and

a course of conduct must involve conduct on at least two occasions.

(4) It shall be a defence to any action of harassment to show that the course of conduct complained of-

    (a) was authorised by, under or by virtue of any enactment or rule of law;

    (b) was pursued for the purpose of preventing or detecting crime; or

    (c) was, in the particular circumstances, reasonable.

(5) In an action of harassment the court may, without prejudice to any other remedies which it may grant-

    (a) award damages;

    (b) grant –

      (i) interdict or interim interdict;

      (ii) if it is satisfied that it is appropriate for it to do so in order to protect the person from further harassment, an order, to be known as a "non-harassment order", requiring the defender to refrain from such conduct in relation to the pursuer as may be specified in the order for such period (which includes an indeterminate period) as may be so specified, but a person may not be subjected to the same prohibitions in an interdict or interim interdict and a non-harassment order at the same time.

(6) The damages which may be awarded in an action of harassment include damages for any anxiety caused by the harassment and any financial loss resulting from it.

(7) Without prejudice to any right to seek review of any interlocutor, a person against whom a non-harassment order has been made, or the person for whose protection the order was made, may apply to the court by which the order was made for revocation of or a variation of the order and, on any such application, the court may revoke the order or vary it in such manner as it considers appropriate.

(8) In section 10(1) of the Damages (Scotland) Act 1976 (interpretation), in the definition of "personal injuries", after "to reputation" there is inserted ", or injury resulting from harassment actionable under section 8 of the Protection from Harassment Act 1997".

Breach of non-harassment order.

9. –

(1) Any person who is found to be in breach of a non-harassment order made under section 8 is guilty of an offence and liable-

    (a) on conviction on indictment, to imprisonment for a term not exceeding five years or to a fine, or to both such imprisonment and such fine; and

    (b) on summary conviction, to imprisonment for a period not exceeding six months or to a fine not exceeding the statutory maximum, or to both such imprisonment and such fine.

(2) A breach of a non-harassment order shall not be punishable other than in accordance with subsection (1).

Limitation.

10. –

(1) After section 18A of the Prescription and Limitation (Scotland) Act 1973 there is inserted the following section-

"Actions of harassment.

18B. –

(1) This section applies to actions of harassment (within the meaning of section 8 of the Protection from Harassment Act 1997) which include a claim for damages.

(2) Subject to subsection (3) below and to section 19A of this Act, no action to which this section applies shall be brought unless it is commenced within a period of 3 years after-

    (a) the date on which the alleged harassment ceased; or

    (b) the date, (if later than the date mentioned in paragraph (a) above) on which the pursuer in the action became, or on which, in the opinion of the court, it would have been reasonably practicable for him in all the circumstances to have become, aware, that the defender was a person responsible for the alleged harassment or the employer or principal of such a person.

(3) In the computation of the period specified in subsection (2) above there shall be disregarded any time during which the person who is alleged to have suffered the harassment was under legal disability by reason of nonage or unsoundness of mind.".

(2) In subsection (1) of section 19A of that Act (power of court to override time-limits), for "section 17 or section 18 and section 18A" there is substituted "section 17, 18, 18A or 18B".

Non-harassment order following criminal offence.

11. After section 234 of the Criminal Procedure (Scotland) Act 1995 there is inserted the following section-

"Non-harassment orders

Non-harassment orders.

234A. –

(1) Where a person is convicted of an offence involving harassment of a person ("the victim"), the prosecutor may apply to the court to make a non-harassment order against the offender requiring him to refrain from such conduct in relation to the victim as may be specified in the order for such period (which includes an indeterminate period) as may be so specified, in addition to any other disposal which may be made in relation to the offence.

(2) On an application under subsection (1) above the court may, if it is satisfied on a balance of probabilities that it is appropriate to do so in order to protect the victim from further harassment, make a non-harassment order.

(3) A non-harassment order made by a criminal court shall be taken to be a sentence for the purposes of any appeal and, for the purposes of this subsection "order" includes any variation or revocation of such an order made under subsection (6) below.

(4) Any person who is found to be in breach of a non-harassment order shall be guilty of an offence and liable-

(a) on conviction on indictment, to imprisonment for a term not exceeding 5 years or to a fine, or to both such imprisonment and such fine; and

(b) on summary conviction, to imprisonment for a period not exceeding 6 months or to a fine not exceeding the statutory maximum, or to both such imprisonment and such fine.

(5) The Lord Advocate, in solemn proceedings, and the prosecutor, in summary proceedings, may appeal to the High Court against any decision by a court to refuse an application under subsection (1) above; and on any such appeal the High Court may make such order as it considers appropriate.

(6) The person against whom a non-harassment order is made, or the prosecutor at whose instance the order is made, may apply to the court which made the order for its revocation or variation and, in relation to any such application the court concerned may, if it is satisfied on a balance of probabilities that it is appropriate to do so, revoke the order or vary it in such manner as it thinks fit, but not so as to increase the period for which the order is to run.

(7) For the purposes of this section "harassment" shall be construed in accordance with section 8 of the Protection from Harassment Act 1997.".

General

National security, etc.

12. –

    (1) If the Secretary of State certifies that in his opinion anything done by a specified person on a specified occasion related to –

        (a) national security,

        (b) the economic well-being of the United Kingdom, or

        (c) the prevention or detection of serious crime, and was done on behalf of the Crown, the certificate is conclusive evidence that this Act does not apply to any conduct of that person on that occasion.

    (2) In subsection (1), "specified" means specified in the certificate in question.

    (3) A document purporting to be a certificate under subsection (1) is to be received in evidence and, unless the contrary is proved, be treated as being such a certificate.

Corresponding provision for Northern Ireland.

13. An Order in Council made under paragraph 1(1)(b) of Schedule 1 to the Northern Ireland Act 1974 which contains a statement that it is made only for purposes corresponding to those of sections 1 to 7 and 12 of this Act –

    (a) shall not be subject to sub-paragraphs (4) and (5) of paragraph 1 of that Schedule (affirmative resolution of both Houses of Parliament), but

    (b) shall be subject to annulment in pursuance of a resolution of either House of Parliament.

Extent

14. –

    (1) Sections 1 to 7 extend to England and Wales only.

    (2) Sections 8 to 11 extend to Scotland only.

    (3) This Act (except section 13) does not extend to Northern Ireland.

Commencement.

15. –

    (1) Sections 1, 2, 4, 5 and 7 to 12 are to come into force on such day as the Secretary of State may by order made by statutory instrument appoint.

    (2) Sections 3 and 6 are to come into force on such day as the Lord Chancellor may by order made by statutory instrument appoint.

    (3) Different days may be appointed under this section for different purposes.

Short title.

16. This Act may be cited as the Protection from Harassment Act 1997.

The Protection from Harassment Act 1997 is reproduced under the terms of Crown Copyright Policy Guidance issued by HMSO.

Appendix 3: Sample restraining order under Protection From Harassment Act 1997

To be used in conjunction with the Rule 2(1) Form of the Magistrates' Courts (Protection from Harassment Restraining Order) Rules 1998

.... Magistrates' Court

.... Code

Date:

Accused:

Address:

Offence: (Section 2/Section 4) Protection from Harassment Act 1997

On .... the accused was convicted of the above offence. For the purpose of protecting the victim .... from further conduct which amounts to harassment or will cause fear of violence, the accused is prohibited from doing anything described in this order.

ORDER: that the accused is prohibited from: –

i) Either by himself / herself or his / her agents directly or indirectly in any way whatsoever from contacting, harassing, alarming, distressing or molesting .... (name).

ii) Notwithstanding the generality of the aforesaid the defendant is prohibited either by himself / herself or his / her agents by any means whatsoever from:

    a) knowingly approach within the boundary of .... (specify street or road names) of any property where he / she knows the said .... to reside, work or frequent.

    b) Telephoning, faxing, or communicating by letter, electronic mail or internet, with the said ...., or the sending or soliciting to send any item or correspondence whatsoever.

    c) From retaining, recording or researching by any means, private, confidential or personal facts or information relating to .... (name).

d) Will not use a different name, or change his / her name without immediately noti-
fying this court (requires also notification of the Crown prosecution Service
and/or the police officer in the Case)
e) Will notify this court of any change of your residence

This ORDER shall remain in existence until further order of the court. (this can mean
life (or any specified period)).

NOTE: BREACH OF THIS ORDER without reasonable excuse IS AN OFFENCE punishable with five years imprisonment.

Copy for defendant:
.... (Defendant's signature)
.... (date)

NOTE: This is only a rough suggestion to invite in depth consideration in relation to
each individual case in preparing a restraining order for inclusion with case file prior to
conviction. Any restrictions may be applied for, and could include family, friends etc.
known to defendant. Similar wording should be considered when an alleged victim is
considering a county court injunction when criminal investigation is not being considered. The wording must be fully considered by the victim, witnesses, family, officer in the
case and CPS before submission and subsequent application to the court.

This is reproduced with permission of the author, DI Ian Smith,
Hampshire Constabulary

Appendix 4: Criminal justice system flow chart, UK

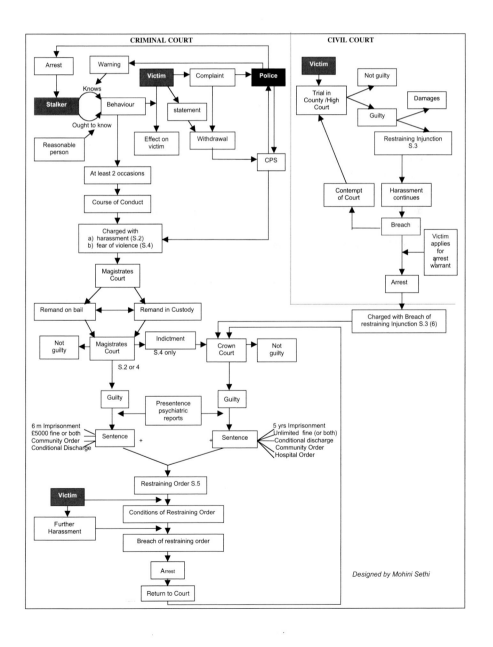

Designed by Mohini Sethi

Index